HAY

Girish Karnad

HAYAVADANA

Translated by the author

OXFORD
UNIVERSITY PRESS

Oxford University Press is a department of the University of Oxford. It furthers the University's objective of excellence in research, scholarship, and education by publishing worldwide. Oxford is a registered trademark of Oxford University Press in the UK and in certain other countries

Published in India by
Oxford University Press
YMCA Library Building, 1, Jai Singh Road, New Delhi 110001, India

First published 1975
35th impression 2016

ISBN-13: 978-0-19-560382-8
ISBN-10: 0-19-560382-6

Printed in India by Magic International Pvt. Ltd., Greater Noida

For

S_______________

INTRODUCTION

Until very recently playwriting in Kannada was a mere literary exercise, with no contact whatever with the living stage. The professional theatre was, as it continues to be, so naïve and rudimentary that both Kailasam and Adya Rangacharya, the two major playwrights in Kannada, rejected it out of hand. But they could not create an enduring substitute for it and were forced to work in isolation.

Fortunately the situation has changed now and a group of young directors and actors have been able to create a theatre which, though entirely dependent on non-professionals, has proved congenial to the growth of new drama. With this new theatre growing around them, new playwrights like Girish Karnad have been able to bring to drama a first-hand knowledge of the practical demands of the stage and a better understanding of dramatic style and technique.

In his works Karnad has moved away from the regionalist tradition that had given Kannada literature its identity in the early years of the century. None of his three plays has a specifically Kannada theme. *Yayati*, his first play, reinterprets an ancient myth. *Tughlaq*, his second play, is based on history. And both the plays are thoroughly modern in outlook and spirit.

The plot of *Hayavadana* comes from *Kathasaritsagara*, an ancient collection of stories in Sanskrit. But Karnad has borrowed it through Thomas Mann's retelling of the story in *The Transposed Heads*. The Sanskrit tale, told by a ghost to an adventurous king, gains a further mock-heroic dimension in Mann's version. The original poses a moral problem while Mann uses it to ridicule the mechanical conception of life which differentiates between body and soul. He ridicules the philosophy which holds the head superior to the body. The human body, Mann argues, is a fit instrument for the fulfilment of human destiny. Even the transposition of heads will not liberate the protagonists from the psychological limits imposed by nature.

Karnad's play poses a different problem, that of human identity in a world of tangled relationships. When the play opens, Devadatta and Kapila are the closest of friends—'one mind, one heart', as the Bhagavata describes them. Devadatta is a man of intellect, Kapila a 'man of the body'. Their relations get complicated when Devadatta marries Padmini. Kapila falls in love with Padmini and she too starts drifting towards him. The friends kill themselves and in a scene, hilariously comic but at the same time full of profound dramatic implications, Padmini transposes their heads, giving Devadatta Kapital's body and Kapila Devadatta's.

The result is a confusion of identities which reveals the ambiguous nature of human personality.

Initially Devadatta—actually the head of Devadatta on Kapila's body—behaves differently from what he was before. But ever so gradually he changes to his former self. So does Kapila. But there is a difference. Devadatta stops writing poetry while Kapila is haunted by the memories in Devadatta's body. Padmini who, after the exchange of heads, had felt that she had the best of both the men, gets slowly disillusioned. Of the three, only she has the capacity for complete experience. She understands but cannot control the situation in which she is placed. Her situation is beautifully summed up by the images of the river and the scarecrows in the choric songs.

A duel that leaves both the friends dead brings the puzzling story to an end. Neither the death of the lovers not the subsequent *suttee* of Padmini is presented as tragic; the deaths serve only to emphasize the logic behind the absurdity of the situation.

The sub-plot of 'Hayavadana', the horse-man, deepens the significance of the main theme of incompleteness by treating it on a different plane. The horse-man's search for completeness ends comically, with his becoming a complete horse. The animal body triumphs over what is considered the best in man, the *Uttamanga*, the human head!

Karnad uses the conventions and motifs of folk tales and folk theatre—masks, curtains, dolls, the story-within-a-story—to create a bizarre world. It is a world of incomplete individuals, indifferent gods, dolls that speak and children who cannot, a world indifferent to the desires and frustrations, joys and sorrows of human beings.

What is real is only the tremendous, irrational energy of the horse and its rider who move round the stage symbolizing the powerful but monotonous rhythm of life.

Karnad has published only three plays so far and it is too early to judge his dramatic achievement. But his work has the tone and expression of great drama. He has the genius and the power to transform any situation into an aesthetic experience, the quality of which, to use Joyce's vocabulary, would be 'static' rather than 'kinetic'. One looks forward to works of greater and more enduring worth.

Vallabh Vidyanagar KIRTINATH KURTKOTI
25 June 1973

NOTE

Hayavadana was originally written in Kannada and I must express my thanks to the Homi Bhabha Fellowships Council for the fellowship which enabled me to write the play.

The central episode in the play—the story of Devadatta and Kapila—is based on a tale from the *Kathasaritsagara*, but I have drawn heavily on Thomas Mann's reworking of the tale in *The Transposed Heads* and am grateful to Mrs Mann for permission to do so.

My special thanks are also due to Mr Rajinder Paul who persuaded me to translate the play into English and first published this translation in his journal, *Enact*.

In translating this play, I have not tried to be consistent while rendering the songs into English. Some have been put in a loose verse form while, for others, only a straightforward prose version has been given.

Girish Karnad

Hayavadana was first presented in English by the Madras Players at the Museum Theatre, Madras on 7 December 1972. The cast was as follows:

S. Ramachander	The Bhagavata
A.V. Dhanushkodi	Actor I/Devadatta
S. Krishnaswamy	Hayavadana
E. Raghukumar	Actor II/Kapila
A. Ratnapapa	Padmini
Vishalam Ekambaram	Doll I
Bhagirathi Narayanan	Doll II
Lakshmi Krishnamurty	Kali
Aman Mittal	Child
Directed by	Lakshmi Krishnamurty Yamuna Prabhu
Music by	B.V. Karanth

ACT ONE

The stage is empty except for a chair, kept centre-stage, and a table on stage right—or at the back—on which the Bhagavata and the musicians sit.

At the beginning of the performance, a mask of Ganesha is brought on stage and kept on the chair. Pooja is done. The Bhagavata sings verses in praise of Ganesha, accompanied by his musicians.

Then the mask is taken away.

O Elephant-headed Herambha
whose flag is victory
and who shines like a thousand suns,
O husband of Riddhi and Siddhi,
seated on a mouse and decorated with a snake,
O single-tusked destroyer of incompleteness,
we pay homage to you and start our play.

BHAGAVATA: May Vighneshwara, the destroyer of obstacles, who removes all hurdles and crowns all endeavours with success, bless our performance now. How indeed can one hope to describe his glory in our poor, disabled words? An elephant's head on a human body, a broken tusk and a cracked belly—whichever way you look at him he seems the embodiment of imperfection, of incompleteness. How indeed can one fathom the mystery that this very Vakratunda-Mahakaya, with his crooked face and distorted body, is the Lord and Master of Success and Perfection? Could it be that this Image of Purity and Holiness, this Mangalamoorty, intends to signify by his very appearance that the completeness of God is something no poor mortal can comprehend? Be that as it may. It is not for us to understand this Mystery or try to unravel it. Nor is it within our powers to do so. Our duty is merely to pay homage to the Elephant-headed god and get on with our play.

This is the city of Dharmapura, ruled by King Dharmasheela whose fame and empire have already reached the ends of the eight directions. Two youths who dwell in this city are our heroes. One is Devadatta. Comely in appearance, fair in colour, unrivalled in intelligence, Devadatta is the only son of the Revered Brahmin, Vidyasagara. Having felled the mightiest pundits of the kingdom in debates on logic and love, having blinded the greatest poets of the world with his poetry and wit, Devadatta is as it were the apple of every eye in Dharmapura.

The other youth is Kapila. He is the only son of the ironsmith, Lohita, who is to the King's armoury as an axle to the chariotwheel. He is dark and plain to look at, yet in deeds which require drive and daring, in dancing, in strength and in physical skills, he has no equal.

(*A scream of terror is heard off-stage. The Bhagavata frowns, quickly looks in the direction of the scream, then carries on.*)

The world wonders at their friendship. The world sees these two young men wandering down the streets of Dharmapura, hand in hand, and remembers Lava and Kusha, Rama and Lakshmana, Krishna and Balarama.

(*Sings.*) Two friends there were
—one mind, one heart—

(*The scream is heard again. The Bhagavata cannot ignore it any more.*)

Who could that be—creating a disturbance at the very outset of our performance? (*Looks.*) Oh—It's Nata, our Actor. And he is running. What could have happened, I wonder?

(*The Actor comes running in, trembling with fear. He rushes on to the stage, runs round the stage once, then sees the Bhagavata and grabs him.*)

ACTOR: Sir, Bhagavata sir—
BHAGAVATA (*trying to free himself*): Tut! Tut! What's this? What's this?
ACTOR: Sir ... oh my God!—God!—
BHAGAVATA: Let me go! I tell you, let go of me!
(*Freeing himself.*) Now what's this? What ...
ACTOR: I—I—I—Oh God! (*Grabs him again.*)
BHAGAVATA: Let me go!
(*The Actor moves back.*)

What nonsense is this? What do you mean by all this shouting and screaming? In front of our audience too! How dare you disturb...

ACTOR: Please, please, I'm—sorry... But—but...

BHAGAVATA (*more calmly*): Now, now, calm down! There's nothing to be afraid of here. I am here. The musicians are here. And there is our large-hearted audience. It may be that they fall asleep during a play sometimes. But they are ever alert when someone is in trouble. Now, tell us, what's the matter?

ACTOR (*panting*): Oh—Oh—My heart... It's going to burst...

BHAGAVATA: Sit down! Sit. Right! Now tell me everything quietly, slowly.

ACTOR: I was on my way here... I was already late... didn't want to annoy you... So I was hurrying down when... Ohh!

(*Covers his face with his hands.*)

BHAGAVATA: Yes, yes. You were hurrying down. Then?

ACTOR: I'm shivering! On the way... you see... I had drunk a lot of water this morning... my stomach was full... so to relieve myself...

BHAGAVATA: Watch what you are saying! Remember you are on stage...

ACTOR: I didn't do anything! I only wanted to... so I sat by the side of the road—and was about to pull up my dhoti when...

BHAGAVATA: Yes?

ACTOR: A voice—a deep, thick voice... It said: 'Hey, you there—don't you know you are not supposed to commit nuisance on the main road?'

BHAGAVATA: Quite right too. You should have known that much.

ACTOR: I half got up and looked around. Not a man in sight—no one! So I was about to sit down again when the same voice said...

BHAGAVATA: Yes?

ACTOR: 'You irresponsible fellow you, can't you understand you are not to commit nuisance on the main road?' I looked up. And there—right in front of me—across the fence...

BHAGAVATA: Who was there?

ACTOR: A horse!

BHAGAVATA: What?

ACTOR: A horse! And it was talking.

BHAGAVATA: What did you have to drink this morning?

ACTOR: Nothing, I swear. Bhagavata sir, I haven't been near a toddy-shop for a whole week. I didn't even have milk today.

BHAGAVATA: Perhaps your liver is sensitive to water.

ACTOR (*desperate*): Please believe me. I saw it clearly—it was a horse—and it was talking.

BHAGAVATA (*resigned*): It's no use continuing this nonsense. So you saw a talking horse? Good. Now go and get made up…

ACTOR: Made up? I fall to your feet, sir, I can't…

BHAGAVATA: Now look here…

ACTOR: Please, sir…

(*He holds up his hand. It's trembling.*)

You see, sir? How can I hold up a sword with this? How can I fight?

BHAGAVATA (*thinks*): Well then. There's only one solution left. You go back…

ACTOR: Back?

BHAGAVATA: …back to that fence, have another look and make sure for yourself that whoever was talking, it couldn't have been that horse.

ACTOR: No!

BHAGAVATA: Nata…

ACTOR: I can't!

BHAGAVATA: It's an order.

ACTOR (*pleading*): Must I?

BHAGAVATA: Yes, you must.

ACTOR: Sir…

(*The Bhagavata turns to the audience and starts singing.*)

BHAGAVATA: Two friends there were
—one mind, one heart—
Are you still here?

(*The Actor goes out looking at the Bhagavata, hoping for a last minute reprieve. It doesn't come.*)

Poor boy! God alone knows what he saw—and what he took it to be! There's Truth for you... Pure Illusion.

(*Sings.*) Two friends there were

—one mind, one heart—

(*A scream in the wings. The Actor comes rushing in.*)

Now look here...

ACTOR: It's coming. Coming...

BHAGAVATA: What's coming?

ACTOR: Him! He's coming... (*Rushes out.*)

BHAGAVATA: Him? It? What's coming? Whatever or whoever it is, the Actor has obviously been frightened by its sight. If even a hardened actor like him gets frightened, it's more than likely that our gentle audience may be affected too. It's not proper to let such a sight walk on stage unchallenged. (*To the wings.*) Hold up the entry-curtain!

(*Two stage-hands enter and hold up a half-curtain, about six feet in height—the sort of curtain used in Yakshatgana or Kathakali. The curtain masks the entry of Hayavadana, who comes and stands behind it.*)

Who's that?

(*No reply. Only the sound of someone sobbing behind the curtain.*)

How strange! Someone's sobbing behind the curtain. It looks as though the Terror which frightened our Actor is itself now crying!

(*To the stage-hand.*) Lower the curtain!

(*The curtain is lowered by about a foot. One sees Hayavadana's head, which is covered by a veil. At a sign from the Bhagavata, one of the stage-hands removes the veil, revealing a horse's head. For a while the horse-head doesn't realize that it is exposed to the gaze of the audience. The moment the realization dawns, the head ducks behind the curtain.*)

BHAGAVATA: A horse! No, it can't be!

(*He makes a sign. The curtain is lowered a little more—just enough to show the head again. Again it ducks. Again the curtain is lowered. This goes on till the curtain is lowered right down to the floor.*

Hayavadana, who has a man's body but a horse's head, is sitting on the floor hiding his head between his knees.)

Incredible! Unbelievable!

(*At a sign from the Bhagavata, the stage-hands withdraw. The Bhagavata goes and stands near Hayavadana. Then he grunts to himself as though he has seen through the trick.*)

Who are you?

(*Hayavadana lifts his head, and wipes the tears away. The Bhagavata beckons to him to come centre-stage.*)

Come here!

(*Hayavadana hesitates, then comes forward.*)

First you go around scaring people with this stupid mask. And then you have the cheek to disturb our show with your clowning? Have you no sense of proportion? ... Enough of this nonsense now. Take it off—I say, take off that stupid mask!

(*Hayavadana doesn't move.*)

You won't?—Then I'll have to do it myself!

(*Holds Hayavadana's head with both his hands and tries to pull it off. Hayavadana doesn't resist.*)

It is tight. Nata—My dear Actor...

(*The Actor comes in, warily, and stands open-mouthed at the sight he sees.*)

Why are you standing there? Don't you see you were taken in by a silly mask? Come and help me take it off now.

(*The Actor comes and holds Hayavadana by his waist while the Bhagavata pulls at the head. Hayavadana offers no resistance, but can't help moaning when the pain becomes unbearable. The tug-of-war continues for a while. Slowly, the truth dawns on the Bhagavata.*)

Nata, this isn't a mask! It's his real head!

(*The Actor drops Hayavadana with a thud. Hayavadana gets up and sits as before, head between knees.*)

Truly, surprises will never cease! If someone had told me only five minutes ago that there existed a man with a horse's head, I would have laughed out in his face.

(*To Hayavadana.*) Who are you?

(*Hayavadana gets up and starts to go out. The Actor hurriedly moves out of his way.*)

Wait! Wait! That's our green room there. It's bad enough that you scared this actor. We have a play to perform today, you know.

(*Hayavadana stands, dejected.*)

(*Softly.*) Who are you?

(*No reply.*)

What brought you to this? Was it a curse of some *rishi*? Or was it some holy place of pilgrimage, a *punyasthana*, which you desecrated? Or could it be that you insulted a *pativrata*, dedicated to the service of her husband? Or did you…

HAYAVADANA: Hey…

BHAGAVATA (*taken aback*): Eh?

HAYAVADANA: What do you mean, Sir? Do you think just because you know the *Puranas* you can go about showering your Sanskrit on everyone in sight? What temple did I desecrate? What woman did I insult? What…

BHAGAVATA: Don't get annoyed…

HAYAVADANA: What else? What *rishi*? What sage? What? Whom have I wronged? What have I done to anyone? Let anyone come forward and say that I've caused him or her any harm. I haven't—I know I haven't. Yet…

(*He is on the point of beginning to sob again.*)

BHAGAVATA: Don't take it to heart so much. What happened? What's your grief? You are not alone here. I am here. The musicians are here. And there is our large-hearted audience. It may be that they fall asleep during a play sometimes…

HAYAVADANA: What can anyone do? It's my fate.

BHAGAVATA: What's your name?

HAYAVADANA: Hayavadana.

BHAGAVATA: How did you get this horse's head?

HAYAVADANA: I was born with it.

BHAGAVATA: Then why didn't you stop us when we tried to take if off? Why did you put up with our torture?

HAYAVADANA: All my life I've been trying to get rid of this head. I thought—you with all your goodness and *punya*… if at least you manage to pull it off…

BHAGAVATA: Oho! Poor man! But, Hayavadana, what can anyone do about a head one's born with? Who knows what error committed in the last birth is responsi…

HAYAVADANA (*annoyed*): It has nothing to do with my last birth. It's this birth which I can't shake off.

BHAGAVATA: Tell us what happened. Don't feel ashamed.

HAYAVADANA (*enraged*): Ashamed? Me? Why should I…

BHAGAVATA: Sorry. I beg your pardon. I should have said 'shy'.

HAYAVADANA (*gloomy*): It's a long story.

BHAGAVATA: Carry on.

HAYAVADANA: My mother was the Princess of Karnataka. She was a very beautiful girl. When she came of age, her father decided that she should choose her own husband. So princes of every kingdom in the world were invited—and they all came. From China, from Persia, from Africa. But she didn't like any of them. The last one to come was the Prince of Araby. My mother took one look at that handsome prince sitting on his great white stallion—and she fainted.

ACTOR: Ah!

HAYAVADANA: Her father at once decided that this was the man. All arrangements for the wedding were made. My mother recovered—and do you know what she said?

ACTOR, BHAGAVATA: What?

HAYAVADANA: She said she would only marry that horse!

ACTOR: What?

HAYAVADANA: Yes. She wouldn't listen to anyone. The Prince of Araby burst a blood-vessel.

ACTOR: Naturally.

HAYAVADANA: No one could dissuade her. So ultimately she was married off to the white stallion. She lived with him for fifteen years. One morning she wakes up—and no horse! In its place stood a beautiful Celestial Being, a *gandharva*. Apparently this Celestial Being had been cursed by the god Kubera to be born a horse for some act of misbehaviour. After fifteen years of human love he had become his original self again.

BHAGAVATA: I must admit several such cases are on record.

HAYAVADANA: Released from his curse, he asked my mother to accompany him to his Heavenly Abode. But she wouldn't. She said she would come only if he became a horse again. So he cursed her…

ACTOR: No!

HAYAVADANA: He cursed her to become a horse herself. So my mother became a horse and ran away prancing happily. My father went back to his Heavenly Abode. Only I—the child of their marriage—was left behind.

BHAGAVATA: It's a sad story.

ACTOR: Very sad.

HAYAVADANA: What should I do now, Bhagavata Sir? What can I do to get rid of this head?

BHAGAVATA: Hayavadana, what's written on our foreheads cannot be altered.

HAYAVADANA (*slapping himself on the forehead*):
But what a forehead! What a forehead! If it was a forehead like yours, I would have accepted anything. But this!… I have tried to accept my fate. My personal life has naturally been blameless. So I took interest in the social life of the Nation—Civics, Politics, Patriotism, Nationalism, Indianization, the Socialist Pattern of Society… I have tried everything. But where's my society? Where? You must help me to become a complete man, Bhagavata Sir. But how? What can I do?

(*Long silence. They think.*)

BHAGAVATA: Banaras?

HAYAVADANA: What?

BHAGAVATA: If you go to Banaras and make a vow in front of the god there…

HAYAVADANA: I've tried that. Didn't work.

BHAGAVATA: Rameshwaram?

HAYAVADANA: Banaras, Rameshwaram, Gokarn, Haridwar, Gaya, Kedarnath—not only those but the *Dargah* of Khwaja Yusuf Baba, the Grotto of Our Virgin Mary—I've tried them all. Magicians, mendicants, maharshis, fakirs, saints and sadhus—sadhus with short hair, sadhus with beards—sadhus in saffron, sadhus in the altogether—hanging, singing, rotating, gyrating—on the spikes, in the air, under water, under the ground—I've covered them all. And what did I get out of all this? Everywhere I went I had to cover my head with a veil—and I started going bald. (*Pause. Shyly.*) You know, I hate this head, but I just can't help being fond of this lovely, long mane. (*Pause.*) So—I had to give the miss to Tirupati.

(*Long silence.*)

BHAGAVATA: Come to think of it, Hayavadana, why don't you try the Kali of Mount Chitrakoot?

HAYAVADANA: Anything you say.

BHAGAVATA: It's temple at the top of Mount Chitrakoot. The goddess there is famous for being ever-awake to the call of the devotees. Thousands used to flock to her temple once. No one goes now, though.

HAYAVADANA: Why not?

BHAGAVATA: She used to give anything anyone asked for. As the people became aware of this, they stopped going.

HAYAVADANA: Fools!

BHAGAVATA: Why don't you try her?

HAYAVADANA (*jumps up*): Why not? I'll start at once...

BHAGAVATA: Good. But I don't think you should go alone. It's a wild road. You'll have to ask a lot of people, which won't be easy for you. So...

(*To the Actor.*) You'd better go with him.

ACTOR: Me?

BHAGAVATA: Yes, that way you can make up for having insulted him.

HAYAVADANA: But, Bhagavata Sir, may I point out that his roadside manners...

ACTOR: There! He's insulting me now! Let him find his own way. What do I care?

BHAGAVATA: Come, come, don't let's start fighting now. (*To Hayavadana.*) Don't worry. There's no highway there. Only a cart-track at best.

(*To the Actor.*) You've no reason to feel insulted. Actually you should admire him. Even in his dire need, he doesn't lose his civic sense. Be off now.

HAYAVADANA (*to the Actor*): Please, don't get upset. I won't bother you, I promise.

(*To the Bhagavata.*) I am most grateful…

BHAGAVATA (*blessing him*): May you become successful in your search for completeness.

(*The two go.*)

Each one to his own fate. Each one to his own desire. Each one to his own luck. Let's now turn to our story.

(*He starts singing. The following is a prose rendering of the song.*)

BHAGAVATA (*sings*): Two friends there were—one mind, one heart. They saw a girl and forgot themselves. But they could not understand the song she sang.

FEMALE CHORUS (*sings*): Why should love stick to the sap of a single body? When the stem is drunk with the thick yearning of the many-petalled, many-flowered lantana, why should it be tied down to the relation of a single flower?

BHAGAVATA (*sings*): They forgot themselves and took off their bodies. And she took the laughing heads, and held them high so the pouring blood bathed her, coloured her red. Then she danced around and sang.

FEMALE CHORUS (*sings*): A head for each breast. A pupil for each eye. A side for each arm. I have neither regret nor shame. The blood pours into the earth and a song branches out in the sky.

(*Devadatta enters and sits on the chair. He is a slender, rather good-looking person with a fair complexion. He is lost in thought. Kapila enters. He is powerfully built and darker.*)

KAPILA (*even as he is entering*): Devadatta, why didn't you come to the gymnasium last evening? I'd asked you to. It was such fun…

DEVADATTA (*preoccupied*): Some work.

KAPILA: Really, you should have come. The wrestler from Gandhara—he's one of India's greatest, you know—he came. Nanda and I were wrestling when he arrived. He watched us. When I caught

Nanda in a crocodile-hold, he first burst into applause and said...

(*Notices that Devadatta isn't listening and stops. Pause.*)

DEVADATTA (*waking up*): Then?

KAPILA: Then what?

DEVADATTA (*flustered*): I mean... what did Nanda do?

KAPILA: He played the flute.

DEVADATTA (*more confused*): No... I mean... you were saying something about the wrestler from Gandhara, weren't you?

KAPILA: He wrestled with me for a few minutes, patted me on the back and said, 'You'll go far.'

DEVADATTA: That's nice.

KAPILA: Yes, it is... Who's it this time?

DEVADATTA: What do you mean?

KAPILA: I mean—who—is—it—this—time?

DEVADATTA: What do you mean who?

KAPILA: I mean—who is the girl?

DEVADATTA: No one. (*Pause.*) How did you guess?

KAPILA: My dear friend, I have seen you fall in love fifteen times in the last two years. How could I not guess?

DEVADATTA: Kapila, if you've come to make fun of me...

KAPILA: I am not making fun of you. Every time, you have been the first to tell me about it. Why so reticent this time?

DEVADATTA: How can you even talk of them in the same breath as her? Before her, they're as...

KAPILA: ... as stars before the moon, as the glow-worms before a torch. Yes, yes, that's been so fifteen times too.

DEVADATTA (*exploding*): Why don't you go home? You are becoming a bore.

KAPILA: Don't get annoyed. Please.

DEVADATTA: You call yourself my friend. But you haven't understood me at all.

KAPILA: And have you understood me? No, you haven't. Or you wouldn't get angry like this. Don't you know I would do anything for you? Jump into a well—or walk into fire? Even my parents aren't as close to me as you are. I would leave them this minute if you asked me to.

DEVADATTA (*irritated*): Don't start on that now. You've said it fifty times already.

KAPILA: ... And I'll say it again. If it wasn't for you I would have been no better than the ox in our yard. You showed me that there were such things as poetry and literature. You taught me...

DEVADATTA: Why don't you go home? All I wanted was to be by myself for a day. Alone. And you had to come and start your chatter. What do you know of poetry and literature? Go back to your smithy—that's where you belong.

KAPILA (*hurt*): Do you really want me to go?

DEVADATTA: Yes.

KAPILA: All right. If that's what you want.

(*He starts to go.*)

DEVADATTA: Sit down.

(*This is of course exactly what Kapila wants. He sits down on the floor.*)

And don't speak...

(*Devadatta gets down on the floor to sit beside Kapila. Kapila at once leaps up and gestures to Devadatta to sit on the chair. Devadatta shakes his head but Kapila insists, pulls him up by his arm. Devadatta gets up.*)

You are a pest.

(*Sits on the chair. Kapila sits down on the ground happily. A long pause.*)

DEVADATTA (*slowly*): How can I describe her, Kapila? Her forelocks rival the bees, her face is ...

(*All this is familiar to Kapila and he joins in, with great enjoyment.*)

BOTH: ... is a white lotus. Her beauty is as the magic lake. Her arms the lotus creepers. Her breasts are golden urns and her waist ...

DEVADATTA: No. No!

KAPILA: Eh?

DEVADATTA: I was blind all these days. I deceived myself that I understood poetry. I didn't. I understood nothing.

Tanvee shyama—

BOTH: ... *shikharidashana pakvabimbadharoshthee—Madhyekshama chakitaharinee prekshana nimnanabhih.*

DEVADATTA: The Shyama Nayika—born of Kalidasa's magic description—as Vatsyayana had dreamt her. Kapila, in a single appearance, she has become my guru in the poetry of love. Do you think she would ever assent to becoming my disciple in love itself?

KAPILA (*aside*): This is new!

DEVADATTA (*his eyes shining*): If only she would consent to be my Muse, I could outshine Kalidasa. I'd always wanted to do that—but I thought it was impossible... But now I see it is within my reach.

KAPILA: Then go ahead. Write ...

DEVADATTA: But how can I without her in front of me? How can I concentrate when my whole being is only thinking of her, craving for her?

KAPILA: What's her name? Will you at least tell me that?

DEVADATTA: Her name? She has no name.

KAPILA: But what do her parents call her?

DEVADATTA (*anguished*): What's the use? She isn't meant for the likes of me...

KAPILA: You don't really believe that, do you? With all your qualities—achievements—looks—family—grace...

DEVADATTA: Don't try to console me with praise.

KAPILA: I'm not praising you. You know very well that every parent of every girl in the city is only waiting to catch you...

DEVADATTA: Don't! Please. I know this girl is beyond my wildest dreams. But still—I can't help wanting her—I can't help it. I swear, Kapila, with you as my witness I swear, if I ever get her as my wife, I'll sacrifice my two arms to the goddess Kali, I'll sacrifice my head to Lord Rudra...

KAPILA Ts! Ts! (*aside*): This is a serious situation. It does look as though this sixteenth girl has really caught our Devadatta in her net. Otherwise, he isn't the type to talk of such violence.

DEVADATTA: I mean it! What's the use of these hands and this head if I'm not to have her? My poetry won't live without her. The *Shakuntalam* will never be excelled. But how can I explain this to her? I have no cloud for a messenger. No bee to show the way. Now the only future I have is to stand and do penance in Pavana Veethi…

KAPILA: Pavana Veethi! Why there?

DEVADATTA: She lives in that street.

KAPILA: How do you know?

DEVADATTA: I saw her in the market yesterday evening. I couldn't remove my eyes from her and followed her home.

KAPILA: Tut! Tut! What must people have thought?

DEVADATTA: She went into a house in Pavana Veethi. I waited outside all evening. She didn't come out.

KAPILA: Now tell me. What sort of a house was it?

DEVADATTA: I can't remember.

KAPILA: What colour?

DEVADATTA: Don't know.

KAPILA: How many storeys?

DEVADATTA: I didn't notice.

KAPILA: You mean you didn't notice anything about the house?

DEVADATTA: The door-frame of the house had an engraving of a two-headed bird at the top. I only saw that. She lifted her hand to knock and it touched the bird. For a minute, the bird came alive.

KAPILA (*jumps up*): Then why didn't you tell me before? You've been wasting precious time…

DEVADATTA: I don't understand…

KAPILA: My dear Devadatta, your cloud-messenger, your bee, your pigeon is sitting right in front of you and you don't even know it? You wait here. I'll go, find out her house, her name…

DEVADATTA (*incredulous*): Kapila—Kapila…

KAPILA: I'll be back in a few minutes…

DEVADATTA: I won't ever forgot this, Kapila…

KAPILA: Shut up! … And forget all about your arms and head. This job doesn't need either Rudra or Kali. I'm quite enough.

(*Goes out.*)

DEVADATTA: Kapila—Kapila . . . He's gone. How fortunate I am to have a friend like him. Pure gold. (*Pause.*) But should I have trusted this to him? He means well—and he is a wizard in his smithy, in his farm, in his fields. But here? No. He is too rough, too indelicate. He was the wrong man to send. He's bound to ruin the whole thing. (*Anguished.*) Lord Rudra, I meant what I said. If I get her, my head will be a gift to you. Mother Kali, I'll sacrifice my arms to you. I swear . . .

(*Goes out. The Bhagavata removes the chair. Kapila enters.*)

KAPILA: This is Pavana Veethi—the street of merchants. Well, well, well. What enormous houses! Each one a palace in itself. It's a wonder people don't get lost in these houses.

(*Examines the doors one by one.*)

Now. This is not a double-headed bird. It's an eagle—This? A lotus. This is—er—a lion. Tiger. A wheel! And this? God alone knows what this is. And the next? (*In disgust.*) A horse!—A rhinoceros—Another lion. Another lotus!—Where the hell is that stupid two-headed bird? (*Stops.*) What was the engraving I couldn't make out? (*Goes back and stares at it. Shouts in triumph.*) That's it! Almost gave me the slip! A proper two-headed bird. But it's so tiny you can't see it at all unless you are willing to tear your eyes staring at it. Well now. Whose house could this be? (*Looks around.*) No one in sight. Naturally. What should anyone come here for in this hot sun? Better ask the people in the house.

(*Mimes knocking. Listens. Padmini enters humming a tune.*)

PADMINI: . . . Here comes the rider—from which land does he come? . . .

KAPILA (*gapes at her. Aside*): I give up, Devadatta. I surrender to your judgement. I hadn't thought anyone could be more beautiful than the wench Ragini who acts Rambha in our village troupe. But this one! You're right—she is Yakshini, Shakuntala, Urvashi, Indumati—all rolled into one.

PADMINI: You knocked, didn't you?

KAPILA: Er—yes . . .

PADMINI: Then why are you gaping at me? What do you want?
KAPILA: I—I just wanted to know whose house this was.
PADMINI: Whose house do you want?
KAPILA: This one.
PADMINI: I see. Then who do you want here?
KAPILA: The master…
PADMINI: Do you know his name?
KAPILA: No.
PADMINI: Have you met him?
KAPILA: No.
PADMINI: Have you seen him?
KAPILA: No.
PADMINI: So. You haven't met him, seen him or known him. What do you want with him?
KAPILA (*aside*): She is quite right. What have I to do with him? I only want to find out his name…
PADMINI: Are you sure you want this house? Or were you…
KAPILA: No. I'm sure this is the one.
PADMINI (*pointing to her head*): Are you all right here?
KAPILA (*taken aback*): Yes—I think so.
PADMINI: How about your eyes? Do they work properly?
KAPILA: Yes.
PADMINI (*showing him four fingers*): How many?
KAPILA: Four.
PADMINI: Correct. So there's nothing wrong with your eyes. As for the other thing, I'll have to take you on trust. Well then. If you are sure you wanted this house, why were you peering at all those doors? And what were you mumbling under your breath?
KAPILA (*startled*): How did you know?
PADMINI: I am quite sane… and I've got good eyes.
KAPILA (*looks up and chuckles*): Oh, I suppose you were watching from the terrace…
PADMINI (*in a low voice, mysteriously*): Listen, you'd better be careful. We have any number of thefts in this street and people are suspicious. Last night there was a man standing out there for nearly two

hours without moving. And today you have turned up. It's just as well I saw you. Anyone else would have taken you to the police. Beware! (*Aloud.*) Now tell me. What are you doing here?

KAPILA: I—I can't tell you.

PADMINI Really! Who will you tell it to?

KAPILA: Your father...

PADMINI: Do you want my father or do you want the master of this house?

KAPILA: Aren't they the same?

PADMINI (*as though explaining to a child*): Listen, my father could be a servant in this house. Or the master of this house could be my father's servant. My father could be the master's father, brother, son-in-law, cousin, grandfather or uncle. Do you agree?

KAPILA: Er—yes.

PADMINI: Right. Then we'll start again. Whom should I call?

KAPILA: Your father.

PADMINI: And if he's not in?

KAPILA (*lost*): Anyone else.

PADMINI: Which anyone?

KAPILA: Perhaps—your brother.

PADMINI: Do you know him?

KAPILA: No.

PADMINI: Have you met him?

KAPILA: No.

PADMINI: Do you know his name?

KAPILA (*desperate*): Please, please—call your father or the master or both, or if they are the same, anyone... please call someone!

PADMINI: No. No. That won't do.

KAPILA (*looking around; aside*): No one here. Still I have to find out her name. Devadatta must be in agony and he will never forgive me if I go back now. (*Aloud.*) Madam, please. I have some very important work. I'll touch your feet...

PADMINI (*eager*): You will? Really? Do you know, I've touched everyone's feet in this house some time or the other, but no one's ever touched mine? You will?

KAPILA (*slapping his forehead as he sinks to the ground*): I'm finished—decimated—powdered to dust—powdered into tiny specks of flour. (*To Padmini.*) My mother, can I at least talk to a servant?

PADMINI: I knew it. I knew you wouldn't touch my feet. One can't even trust strangers any more. All right, my dear son! I opened the door. So consider me the door-keeper. What do you want?

KAPILA (*determined*): All right! (*Gets up.*) You have no doubt heard of the Revered Brahmin Vidyasagara.

PADMINI: It's possible.

KAPILA: In which case you'll also know of Devadatta, his only son. A poet. A pundit. Knows the Vedas backwards. Writes the grandest poetry ever. Long, dark hair. Delicate, fair face. Age twenty. Height five feet seven inches. Weight...

PADMINI: Wait a minute! What's he to you?

KAPILA: Friend. Greatest in the world! But the main question now is: What's he going to be to you?

(*Sudden silence.*)

PADMINI (*blushing as the import of the remark dawns on her*): Mother!

(*Runs in. Kapila stands, staring after her.*)

KAPILA: Devadatta, my friend, I confess to you I'm feeling uneasy. You are a gentle soul. You can't bear a bitter word or an evil thought. But this one is fast as lightning—and as sharp. She is not for the likes of you. What she needs is a man of steel. But what can one do? You'll never listen to me. And I can't withdraw now. I'll have to talk to her family...

(*Follows her in.*)

BHAGAVATA: Need one explain to our wise and knowing audience what followed next? Padmini is the daughter of the leading merchant in Dharmapura. In her house, the very floor is swept by the Goddess of Wealth. In Devadatta's house, they've the Goddess of Learning for a maid. What could then possibly stand in the way of bringing the families together? (*Marriage music.*) Padmini became the better half of Devadatta and settled in his house. Nor did Devadatta forget his debt to Kapila. The old friendship flourished as before. Devadatta—Padmini—Kapila! To the admiring citizens of Dharmapura, Rama—Sita—Lakshmana.

(*Enter Devadatta and Padmini.*)

PADMINI: Why is he so late? He should have been here more than an hour ago.

(*Looks out of a window.*)

DEVADATTA: Have you packed your clothes properly?

PADMINI: The first thing in the morning.

DEVADATTA: And the mattresses? We may have to sleep out in the open. It's quite chilly. We'll need at least two rugs.

PADMINI: Don't worry. The servant's done all that.

DEVADATTA: And your shawl? Also some warm clothes...

PADMINI: What's happened to you today? At other times you are so full of your books, you even forget to wash your hands after a meal. But today you've been going on and on and on all morning.

DEVADATTA: Padmini, I've told you ten times already I don't like the idea of this trip. You should rest—not face such hazards. The cart will probably shake like an earthquake. It's dangerous in your condition. But you won't listen.

PADMINI: My condition! What's happened to me? To listen to you, one would think I was the first woman in this world to become pregnant. I only have to stumble and you act as though it's all finished and gone...

DEVADATTA: For God's sake, will you stop it?

PADMINI (*laughs*): Sorry! (*Bites her tongue in repentance.*) I won't say such things again.

DEVADATTA: You've no sense of what not to say. So long as you can chatter and run around like a child...

PADMINI (*back at the window*): Where is Kapila?

DEVADATTA: ... and drool over Kapila all day.

PADMINI (*taken aback*): What do you mean?

DEVADATTA: What else should I say? The other day I wanted to read out a play of Bhasa's to you and sure enough Kapila drops in.

PADMINI: Oh! That's biting you still, is it? But why are you blaming me? He was your friend even before you married me, wasn't he? He used to drop in every day even then…

DEVADATTA: But shouldn't he realize I'm a married man now? He just can't go on as before…

PADMINI: Don't blame him. It's my fault. He learnt a bit about poetry from you and I thought he might enjoy Bhasa. So I asked him to come. He didn't want to but I insisted.

DEVADATTA: I know that.

PADMINI: Had I realized you would be so upset, I wouldn't have.

DEVADATTA: I'm not upset, Padmini. Kapila isn't merely a friend—he's like my brother. One has to collect merit in seven lives to get a friend like him. But is it wrong for me to want to read to you alone? Or to spend a couple of days with you without anyone else around? (*Pause.*) Of course, once he came, there wasn't the slightest chance of my reading any poetry. You had to hop around him twittering 'Kapila! Kapila!' every minute.

PADMINI: You aren't jealous of him, are you?

DEVADATTA: Me? Jealous of Kapila? Why do you have to twist everything I say…

PADMINI (*laughs. Affectionately*): Don't sulk now. I was just trying to be funny. Really you have no sense of humour.

DEVADATTA: It's humour for you. But it burns my insides.

PADMINI: Aw, shut up. Don't I know how liberal and largehearted you are? You aren't the sort to get jealous. If I were to fall into a well tomorrow, you wouldn't even miss me until my bloated corpse floated up…

DEVADATTA (*irritated*): Padmini!

PADMINI: Sorry, I forgot. I apologize—I slap myself on the cheeks. (*Slaps herself on both cheeks with her right hand several times in punishment.*) Is that all right? The trouble is I grew up saying these awful things and it's become a habit now. But you are so fragile! I don't know how you're going to go through life wrapped in silk like this! You are still a baby…

DEVADATTA: I see.

PADMINI: Look now. You got annoyed about Kapila. But why? You are my saffron, my marriage thread, my deity. Why should you feel disturbed? I like making fun of Kapila—he is such an innocent. Looks a proper devil, but the way he blushes and giggles and turns red, he might have been a bride.

DEVADATTA (*smiles*): Well, this bride didn't blush.

PADMINI: No one taught this bride to blush. But now I'm learning from that yokel.

(*They both laugh. She casually goes back to the window and looks out.*)

DEVADATTA (*aside*): Does she really not see? Or is she deliberately playing this game with him? Kapila was never the sort to blush. But now, he only has to see her and he begins to wag his tail. Sits up on his hind legs as though he were afraid to let her words fall to the ground. And that pleading in his eyes—can't she really see that? (*Aloud.*) Padmini, Kapila isn't used to women. The only woman he has known in his life is his mother.

PADMINI: You mean it's dangerous to be with him? The way you talk one would never imagine he was your best friend.

DEVADATTA (*incensed*): Why do you have to twist everything I say…

PADMINI (*conciliatory*): What did I say? Listen, if you really don't want to go to Ujjain today, let's not. When Kapila comes, tell him I'm ill.

DEVADATTA: But … you will be disappointed.

PADMINI: Me? Of course not. We'll do as you feel. You remember what the priest said—I'm your 'half' now. The better half! We can go to Ujjain some other time… In another couple of months, there's the big Ujjain fair. We'll go then—just the two of us. All right? We'll cancel today's trip.

DEVADATTA (*trying to control his excitement*): Now—if you aren't going to be disappointed—then—truly—that's what I would like most. Not because I'm jealous of Kapila—No, I'm not, I know that. He has a heart of gold. But this is your first baby…

PADMINI: What do you mean first? How many babies can one have within six months?

DEVADATTA: You aren't going to start again?

PADMINI: No, no, no, I won't say a word.

DEVADATTA (*pinching her cheek*): Bad upbringing—that's what it is. I don't like the idea of your going out in a cart in your present condition, that's all.

PADMINI: Ordinarily I would have replied I had a womb of steel, but I won't—in the present condition.

(*Both laugh.*)

All right. If you are happy, so am I.

DEVADATTA (*happy*): Yes, we'll spend the whole day by ourselves. The servants are going home anyway. They can come back tomorrow. But for today—only you and me. It's been such a long time since we've been on our own.

KAPILA (*off-stage*): Devadatta…

PADMINI: There's Kapila now. You tell him.

(*She pretends to go in, but goes and stands in a corner of the stage, listening. Kapila enters excited.*)

KAPILA: I'm late, ain't I? What could I do? That cartman had kept the cart ready but the moment I looked at it, I knew one of the oxen was no good. I asked him to change it. 'We won't reach Ujjain for another fortnight in this one,' I said. He started…

DEVADATTA: Kapila…

KAPILA: … making a scene, but I stood my ground. So he had to fetch a new one. These cart-hirers are a menace. If ours hadn't gone to Chitrapur that day…

DEVADATTA: Kapila, we have to call off today's trip.

KAPILA (*suddenly silenced*): Oh!

DEVADATTA (*embarrassed*): You see, Padmini isn't well…

KAPILA: Well, then of course…

(*Silence.*)

I'll return the cart then.

DEVADATTA: Yes.

KAPILA: Or else he may charge us for the day.

DEVADATTA: Uhm.

KAPILA (*aside*): So it's off. What am I to do for the rest of the day? What am I to do for the rest of the week? Why should it feel as though the whole world has been wiped out for a whole week? Why this emptiness? Kapila, Kapila, get a tight hold on yourself. You are slipping, boy, control yourself. Don't lose that hold. Go now. Don't come here again for a week. Devadatta's bound to get angry with you for not visiting. Sister-in-law will be annoyed. But don't come back. Go, Go! (*Aloud*.) Well then—I'll start.

DEVADATTA: Why don't you sit for a while?

KAPILA: No, no. We might upset sister-in-law more then with our prattle.

DEVADATTA: That's true. So come again. Soon.

KAPILA: Yes, I will.

(*Starts to go. Padmini comes out*.)

PADMINI: Why are you sitting here? When are we going to start? We are already late...

(*They look at her, surprised*.)

KAPILA: But if you aren't well, we won't...

PADMINI: What's wrong with me? I'm in perfect health. I had a headache this morning. But a layer of ginger paste took care of that. Why should we cancel our trip for a little thing like that?

(*Devadatta opens his mouth to say something but stays quiet*.)

(*To Kapila*.) Why are you standing there like a statue?

KAPILA: No, really, if you have a headache...

PADMINI: I don't have a headache now!

DEVADATTA: But, Padmini ...

PADMINI: Kapila, put those bundles out there in the cart. The servant will bring the rest.

(*Kapila stands totally baffled. He looks at Devadatta for guidance. There's none*.)

Be quick. Otherwise I'll put them in myself.

(*Kapila goes out. Padmini goes to Devadatta. Pleading*.)

Please don't get angry. Poor boy, he looked so lost and disappointed, I couldn't bear to see it. He has been running around for us this whole week.

DEVADATTA (*turning his head away*): Where's the box in which I put the books? Let me take it.

PADMINI: You are an angel. I knew you wouldn't mind. I'll bring it. It's quite light.

(*Goes out.*)

DEVADATTA (*to himself*): And my disappointment? Does that mean nothing to you? (*Aloud.*) Don't. I'll take it. Please, don't lift anything.

(*Goes in after her.*)

BHAGAVATA: Why do you tremble, heart? Why do you cringe like a touch-me-not bush through which a snake has passed? The sun rests his head on the Fortunate Lady's flower.

And the head is bidding good-bye to the heart.

(*Kapila, followed by Padmini and Devadatta, enters miming a cart-ride. Kapila is driving the cart.*)

PADMINI: How beautifully you drive the cart, Kapila! Your hands don't even move, but the oxen seem to know exactly which way you want them to go.

(*Kapila laughs happily.*)

Shall we stop here for a while? We've been in this cart all day and my legs feel like bits of wood.

KAPILA: Right! Ho—Ho...

(*Pulls the cart to a halt. They get down. She slips but Devadatta supports her.*)

PADMINI: What a terrible road. Nothing but potholes and rocks. But one didn't feel a thing in the cart! You drove it so gently—almost made it float. I remember when Devadatta took me in a cart. That was soon after our marriage. I insisted on being shown the lake outside the city. So we started, only the two of us and Devadatta driving—against my advice, I must say. And we didn't even cross the city-gates. The oxen took everything except the road. He only had to pull to the right, and off they would rush to the left! I've never laughed so much in my life. But of course he got very angry, so we had to go back home straight!

(*Laughs. But Kapila and Devadatta don't join in.*)

Kapila, what's that glorious tree there? That one, covered with flowers?

KAPILA: Oh that! That's called the Fortunate Lady's flower—that means a married woman...

PADMINI: I know! But why do they call it that?

KAPILA: Wait. I'll bring you a flower. Then you'll see.

(*Goes out.*)

PADMINI (*watching him, aside*): How he climbs—like an ape. Before I could even say 'yes', he had taken off his shirt, pulled his *dhoti* up and swung up the branch. And what an ethereal shape! Such a broad back: like an ocean with muscles rippling across it—and then that small, feminine waist which looks so helpless.

DEVADATTA (*aside*): She had so much to talk about all day, she couldn't wait for breath. Now, not a word.

PADMINI (*aside*): He is like a Celestial Being reborn as a hunter. How his body sways, his limbs curve—It's a dance almost.

DEVADATTA (*aside*): And why should I blame her? It's his strong body—his manly muscles. And to think I had never *ever* noticed them all these years! I was an innocent—an absolute baby.

PADMINI (*aside*): No woman could resist him.

DEVADATTA (*aside*): No woman could resist him—and what does it matter that she's married? What a fool I've been. All these days I only saw that pleading in his eyes stretching out its arms, begging for a favour. But never looked in her eyes. And when I did, took the whites of her eyes for their real depth. Only now I see the depths. Now I see these flames leaping up from those depths. Now! So late! Don't turn away now, Devadatta, look at her. Look at those yellow, purple flames. Look how she's pouring her soul into his mould. Look! Let your guts burn out. Let your lungs turn to ash, but don't turn away. Look and don't scream. Strangle your agony. But look deep into these eyes—look until those peacock flames burn out the blindness in you. Don't be a coward now.

PADMINI (*aside*): How long can one go on like this? How long? How long? If Devadatta notices...

(*Looks at Devadatta. He is looking at her already and their eyes meet. Both look away.*)

PADMINI (*aloud*): There he comes. All I wanted was one flower and he's brought a heap.

(*Kapila comes in, miming a whole load of flowers in his arms and hands. He pours them out in front of her.*)

KAPILA: Here you are. The Fortunate Lady's flowers.

PADMINI: And why a 'Fortunate Lady', pray?

KAPILA: Because it has all the marks of marriage a woman puts on. The yellow on the petals. Then that red round patch at the bottom of the petals, like on your foreheads. Then, here, that thin saffron line, like in the parting of your hair. Then—uhm ... oh yes—here near the stem a row of black dots, like a necklace of black beads—

PADMINI: What imagination! (*To Devadatta.*) You should put it in your poetry. It's good for a simile.

DEVADATTA: Shall we go? It's quite late.

PADMINI: Let's stay. I have been sitting in that cart for I don't know how long. I didn't know the road to Ujjain was so enchanting.

KAPILA: The others take a longer route. This is a more wooded area, so very few come this way. But I like this better. Besides, it's fifteen miles shorter.

PADMINI: I wouldn't have minded even if it were fifteen miles longer. It's like a garden.

KAPILA: Isn't it? Look there, do you see it? That's the river Bhargavi. The poet Vyasa had a hermitage on its banks. There's a temple of Rudra there now.

DEVADATTA (*suddenly awake*): A temple of Rudra?

KAPILA: Yes, It's beautiful. And—there—beyond that hill is a temple of Kali.

(*Two stage-hands come and hold up a half-curtain in the corner to which he points. The curtain has a picture of Goddess Kali on it. The Bhagavata places a sword in front of it.*)

It was very prosperous once. But now it's quite dilapidated.

DEVADATTA (*as though in a trance*): The temple of Rudra!

KAPILA: Yes, that's old too. But not half as ruined as the Kali temple. We can have a look if you like.

PADMINI: Yes, let's.

DEVADATTA: Why don't you go and see the Kali temple first?

KAPILA: No, that's quite terrible. I saw it once: bats, snakes, all sorts of poisonous insects—and no proper road. We can go to the Rudra temple, though. It's nearer.

PADMINI: Come on. Let's go.

DEVADATTA: You two go. I won't come.

PADMINI (*pause*): And you?

DEVADATTA: I'll stay here and watch the cart.

KAPILA: But there's no fear of thieves here. (*Sensing the tension.*) Or else. I'll stay here.

DEVADATTA: No, no. You two go. I'm also a little tired.

PADMINI (*aside*): He has started it again. Another tantrum. Let him. What do I care? (*Aloud.*) Come, Kapila, we'll go.

KAPILA: But perhaps in your condition...

PADMINI (*exploding*): Why are you two hounding me with this condition? If you don't want to come, say so. Don't make excuses...

KAPILA: Devadatta, it's not very far. You come too.

DEVADATTA: I told you to go. Don't force me, please.

PADMINI: Let's not go. I don't want the two of you to suffer for my sake.

DEVADATTA (*to Kapila*): Go.

KAPILA (*he has no choice*): Come. We'll be back soon.

(*Kapila and Padmini go out.*)

DEVADATTA: Good-bye, Kapila. Good-bye, Padmini. May Lord Rudra bless you. You are two pieces of my heart—Live happily together. I shall find my eternal happiness in that thought. (*Agonized.*) Give me strength, Lord Rudra. My father, give me courage. I'm already trembling, I'd never thought I would be so afraid. Give me courage, Father, strengthen me.

(*He walks to the temple of Kali. It's a steep and difficult climb. He is exhausted by the time he reaches the temple. He prostrates himself before the goddess.*)

Bhavani, Bhairavi, Kali, Durga, Mahamaya, Mother of all Nature, I had forgotten my promise to you. Forgive me, Mother. You fulfilled the deepest craving of my life. You gave me Padmini—and I forgot my word. Forgive me, for I'm here now to carry out my promise.

(*Picks up the sword.*)

Great indeed is your mercy. Even in this lonely place some devotee of yours—a hunter perhaps or a tribesman—has left this weapon. Who knows how many lives this weapon has sacrificed to you. (*Screaming.*) Here, Mother Kali, here's another. My head. Take it, Mother, accept this little offering of my head.

(*Cuts off his head. Not an easy thing to do. He struggles, groans, writhes. Ultimately succeeds in killing himself.*

A long silence. Padmini and Kapila return to the cart.)

PADMINI (*enters talking*): ... he should have come. How thrilling it was! Heavenly! But of course he has no enthusiasm for these things. After all...

(*Notices Devadatta isn't there.*)

Where's Devadatta?

(*They look around.*)

He said he'd stay here!

KAPILA (*calls*): Devadatta—Devadatta—

PADMINI: He's probably somewhere around. Where will he go? He has the tenderest feet on earth. They manage to get blisters, corns, cuts, boils and wounds without any effort.

KAPILA (*calls*): Devadatta.

PADMINI: Why are you shouting? Sit down. He'll come.

(*Kapila inspects the surrounding area. Gives a gasp of surprise.*)

What's it?

KAPILA: His footprints. He has obviously gone in that direction. (*Pause.*) But—that's where the Kali temple is!

PADMINI: You don't mean he's gone there! How absurd!

KAPILA: You stay here. I'll bring him back.

PADMINI: But why do you have to go? There's nothing to fear in this broad daylight!

KAPILA (*hurrying off*): It's very thickly wooded there. If he gets lost, he'll have to spend the whole night in the jungle. You stay here. I'll come back in no time.

(*Runs out.*)

PADMINI (*exasperated*): He's gone! Really, he seems more worried about Devadatta than me.

(*She sits down. Kapila goes to the Kali temple—but naturally faster than Devadatta did. He sees the body and his mouth half opens in a scream. He runs to Devadatta and kneels beside him. Lifts his truncated head and moans.*)

KAPILA: You've cut off your head! You've cut off your head! Oh my dear friend, my brother, what have you done? Were you so angry with me? Did you feel such contempt for me, such abhorrence? And in your anger you forgot that I was ready to die for you? If you had asked me to jump into fire, I would have done it. If you had asked me to leave the country, I would have done it. If you had asked me to go and drown in a river, I would have accepted. Did you despise me so much that you couldn't ask me that? I did wrong. But you know I don't have the intelligence to know what else I should have done. I couldn't think—and so you've pushed me away? No, Devadatta, I can't live without you. I can't breathe without you. Devadatta, my brother, my guru, my friend…

(*Picks up the sword.*)

You spurned me in this world. Accept me as your brother at least in the next. Here, friend, here I come. As always, I follow in your footsteps.

(*Cuts off his head. It's an easier death this time. Padmini, who has been still till now, moves.*)

PADMINI: Where are they? Now Kapila's disappeared too. He couldn't still be searching for him. That's not possible. Devadatta's too weak to have gone far. They must have met. Perhaps they're sitting now, chatting as in the old days. For once, no bother of a wife around. No, more likely Devadatta's sulking. He's probably tearing poor Kapila to shreds by just being silent and grumpy. Yes, that would be more like him.

(*Pause.*)

It's almost dark. And they aren't back. Shameless men—to leave me alone like this here!

No, it's no use sitting here any longer. I had better go and look for them. If I die of a snake-bite on the way, serve them right. Or perhaps, so much the better for them.

(*Walks to the temple, slowly. Rubs her eyes when she reaches there.*)

How dark it is! Can't see a thing. (*Calls.*) Kapila—Kapila—Devadatta isn't here either. What shall I do here? At this time of the night! Alone! (*Listens.*) What's that? Some wild beast. A hyena! It's right outside—what shall I do if it comes in? Ah! It's gone. Mother Kali, only you can protect me now.

(*Stumbles over the bodies.*)

What's this? What's this?

(*Stares at the bodies and then lets out a terrified scream.*)

Oh God! What's this? Both! Both gone! And didn't even think of me before they went? What shall I do? What shall I do? Oh, Devadatta, what did I do that you left me alone in this state? Was that how much you loved me? And you, Kapila, who looked at me with dog's eyes, you too? How selfish you are, you men, and how thoughtless! What shall I do now? Where shall I go? How can I go home?

(*Pause.*)

Home? And what shall I say when I get there? What shall I say happened? And who'll believe me? They'll all say the two fought and died for this whore. They're bound to say it. Then what'll happen to me? No, Mother Kali, no, it's too horrible to think of. No! Kapila's gone, Devadatta's gone. Let me go with them.

(*Picks up the sword.*)

I don't have the strength to hack off my head. But what does it matter how I die, Mother? You don't care. It's the same to you—another offering! All right. Have it then. Here's another offering for you.

(*Lifts the sword and puts its point on her breast when, from behind the curtain, the goddess's voice is heard.*)

VOICE: Hey…
(Padmini freezes.)
Put it down! Put down that sword!
(*Padmini jumps up in fright and, throwing the sword aside, tries to run out of the temple. Then stops.*)
PADMINI: Who's that?
(*No reply.*)
Who's that?
(*A tremendous noise of drums. Padmini shuts her eyes in terror. Behind the curtain one sees the uplifted blood-red palms of the goddess. The curtain is lowered and taken away and one sees a terrifying figure, her arms stretched out, her mouth wide open with the tongue lolling out. The drums stop and as the goddess drops her arms and shuts her mouth, it becomes clear she has been yawning.*)
KALI (*completes the yawn*): All right. Open your eyes and be quick. Don't waste time.
(*Padmini opens her eyes and sees the goddess. She runs and falls at her feet.*)
PADMINI: Mother—Kali…
KALI (*sleepy*): Yes, it's me. There was a time—many years ago—when at this hour they would have the *mangalarati*. The devotees used to make a deafening racket with drums and conch-shells and cymbals. So I used to be wide awake around now. I've lost the habit. (*Yawns.*) Right. What do you want? Tell me. I'm pleased with you.
PADMINI: Save me, Mother…
KALI: I know. I've done that already.
PADMINI: Do you call this saving, Mother of all Nature? I can't show my face to anyone in the world. I can't…
KALI (*a little testily*): Yes, yes, you've said that once. No need to repeat yourself. Now do as I tell you. Put these heads back properly. Attach them to their bodies and then press that sword on their necks. They'll come up alive. Is that enough?
PADMINI: Mother, you are our breath, you are our bread—and—water…

KALI: Skip it! Do as I told you. And quickly. I'm collapsing with sleep.

PADMINI (*hesitating*): May I ask a question?

KALI: If it's not too long.

PADMINI: Can there ever be anything you don't already know, Mother? The past and the future are mere specks in your palm. Then why didn't you stop Devadatta when he came here? Why didn't you stop Kapila? If you'd saved either of them, I would have been spared all this terror, this agony. Why did you wait so long?

KALI (*surprised*): Is that all you can think of now?

PADMINI: Mother...

KALI: I've never seen anyone like you.

PADMINI: How could one possibly hide anything from you, Mother?

KALI: That's true enough.

PADMINI: Then why didn't you stop them?

KALI: Actually if it hadn't been that I was so sleepy, I would have thrown them out by the scruff of their necks.

PADMINI: But why?

KALI: The rascals! They were lying to their last breaths. That fellow Devadatta—he had once promised his head to Rudra and his arms to me! Think of it—head to him and arms to me! Then because you insisted on going to the Rudra temple, he comes here and offers his head. Nobly too—wants to keep his word, he says—no other reason!

Then this Kapila, died right in front of me—but 'for his friend'. Mind you! Didn't even have the courtesy to refer to me. And what lies! Says he is dying for friendship. He must have known perfectly well he would be accused of killing Devadatta for you. Do you think he wouldn't have grabbed you if it hadn't been for that fear? But till his last breath—'Oh my friend! My dear brother!'

Only you spoke the truth.

PADMINI: It's all your grace, Mother...

KALI: Don't drag me into it. I had nothing to do with it. You spoke the truth because you're selfish, that's all. Now don't go on. Do what I told you and shut your eyes.

PADMINI: Yes, Mother…

(*Eagerly, Padmini attaches the severed heads to the bodies of the men. But in her excitement she mixes them up so that Devadatta's head goes to Kapila's body and vice versa. Then presses the sword on their necks, does* namaskara *to the goddess, walks downstage and stands with her back to the goddess, her eyes shut tight.*)

PADMINI: I'm ready, Mother.

KALI (*in a resigned tone*): My dear daughter, there should be a limit even to honesty. Anyway, so be it!

(*Again the drums. The curtain is held up again and the goddess disappears behind it. During the following scene, the stage-hands, the curtain as well as the goddess leave the stage.*

Padmini stands immobile with her eyes shut. The drums stop. A long silence follows. The dead bodies move. Their breathing becomes loud and laboured. They sit up, slowly, stiffly. Their movement is mechanical, as though blood-circulation has not started properly yet. They feel their own arms, heads and bodies, and look around, bewildered.

Henceforth the person with the head of Devadatta will be called Devadatta. Similarly with Kapila.

They stand up. It's not easy and they reel around a bit.

Padmini is still.)

DEVADATTA: What—happened?

KAPILA: What happened?

(*Padmini opens her eyes, but she still doesn't dare to look at them.*)

PADMINI: Devadatta's voice! Kapila's voice!

(*Screaming with joy.*) Kapila! Devadatta!

(*Turns and runs to them. Then suddenly stops and stands paralysed.*)

KAPILA: Who …?

DEVADATTA: Padmini?

KAPILA: What—happened? My head—Ooh! It feels so heavy!

DEVADATTA: My body—seems to weigh—a ton.

PADMINI (*running around in confusion*): What have I done? What have I done? What have I done? Mother Kali, only you can save me now—only you can help me—What have I done? What have I done? What should I do? Mother, Mother…

DEVADATTA (*a little more alive*): Why are you—crying?

KAPILA: What's—wrong?

PADMINI: What shall I tell you, Devadatta? How can I explain it, Kapila? You cut off your heads. But the goddess gave you life—but—I—I—in the dark... Mother, only you can protect me now—Mother! I—mixed up your heads—I mixed them up! Forgive me—I don't deserve to live—forgive me...

KAPILA (*looking at Devadatta*): You mixed up...

DEVADATTA: ... the heads?

(*They stare at each other. Then burst into laughter. She doesn't know how to react. Watches them. Then starts laughing.*)

DEVADATTA: Mixed-up heads!

KAPILA: Heads mixed-up!

DEVADATTA: Exchanged heads!

KAPILA: Heads exchanged!

DEVADATTA: How fantastic! All these years we were only friends!

KAPILA: Now we are blood-relations! Body-relations! (*Laughing.*) What a gift!

DEVADATTA: Forgive you? We must thank you...

KAPILA: We'll never be able to thank you—enough...

DEVADATTA: Exchanged heads!

(*They roar with laughter. Then all three hold hands and run round in a circle, singing.*)

ALL THREE (*together*):

> What a good mix!
> No more tricks!
> Is this one that
> Or that one this?
> Ho! Ho!

(*They sing this over and over again until they collapse on the floor.*)

KAPILA: Oooh—I'm finished!

PADMINI: ... Dead!

DEVADATTA: Nothing like this could have ever happened before.

PADMINI: You know, seeing you two with your heads off was bad enough. But when you got up it was terrible! I almost died of fright…

(*They laugh.*)

KAPILA: No one will believe us if we tell them.

PADMINI (*suddenly*): We won't tell anyone.

DEVADATTA: We'll keep our secrets inside us.

PADMINI: 'Inside us' is right.

(*Laughter.*)

KAPILA: But how can we not tell? They'll know soon…

DEVADATTA: No one'll know.

KAPILA: I'm sure they'll…

DEVADATTA: I'll take any bet.

KAPILA: But how's that possible?

DEVADATTA: You'll see. Why worry now?

PADMINI: Come. Let's go.

KAPILA: It's late.

DEVADATTA: No Ujjain now. We go back home!

KAPILA: Absolutely.

PADMINI: This Ujjain will last us a lifetime. Come.

(*They get up. Every now and then someone laughs and then all burst out together.*)

PADMINI: Devadatta, I really don't know how we're going to keep this from your parents. They'll guess as soon as they see you bare-bodied.

DEVADATTA: They won't, I tell you. They take us too much for granted.

KAPILA: What do you mean?

DEVADATTA: Who ever pays attention to a person he sees every day?

KAPILA: I don't mean that…

PADMINI: I'm not so sure. I'm afraid I'll get the blame for it ultimately.

DEVADATTA: Stop worrying! I tell you it…

KAPILA: But what has she got to do with you now?

DEVADATTA (*stops*): What do you mean?

KAPILA: I mean Padmini must come home with me, shouldn't she? She's my wife, so she must...

(*Exclamations from Devadatta and Padmini.*)

PADMINI: What are you talking about, Kapila?

KAPILA (*explaining*): I mean, you are Devadatta's wife. I have Devadatta's body now. So you have to be my wife.

PADMINI: Shut up!

DEVADATTA: Don't blather like an idiot! I am Devadatta...

PADMINI: Aren't you ashamed of yourself?

KAPILA: But why, Padmini? I have Devadatta's body now...

DEVADATTA: We know that. You don't have to repeat yourself like a parrot. According to the Shastras, the head is the sign of a man...

KAPILA (*angry now*): That may be. But the question now is simply this: Whose wife is she? (*Raising his right hand.*) This is the hand that accepted her at the wedding. This the body she's lived with all these months. And the child she's carrying is the seed of this body.

PADMINI (*frightened by the logic*): No, no, no. It's not possible. It's not. (*Running to Devadatta.*) It's not, Devadatta.

DEVADATTA: Of course, it isn't, my dear. He is ignorant. (*To Kapila.*) When one accepts a partner in marriage, with the holy fire as one's witness, one accepts a person, not a body. She didn't marry Devadatta's body, she married Devadatta—the person.

KAPILA: If that's your argument, I have Devadatta's body, so I am Devadatta—the person.

DEVADATTA: Listen to me. Of all the human limbs the topmost—in position as well as in importance—is the head. I have Devadatta's head and it follows that I am Devadatta. According to the Sacred Texts...

KAPILA: Don't tell me about your Sacred Texts. You can always twist them to suit your needs. She married Devadatta's body with the holy fire as her witness and that's enough for me.

DEVADATTA (*laughs*): Did you hear that, Padmini? He claims to be Devadatta and yet he scorns the Texts. You think Devadatta would ever do that?

KAPILA: You can quote as many Texts as you like, I don't give a nail. Come on, Padmini…

(*Takes a step towards her. But Devadatta steps in between.*)

DEVADATTA: Take care!

PADMINI: Come, Devadatta. It's no use arguing with this rascal. Let's go.

DEVADATTA: Come on.

KAPILA (*stepping between them*): Where are you taking my wife, friend?

DEVADATTA: Will you get out of our way or should…

KAPILA: It was you who got in my way.

DEVADATTA (*pushing Kapila aside*): Get away, you pig.

KAPILA (*triumphant*): He's using force! And what language! Padmini, think! Would Devadatta ever have acted like this? This is Kapila's violence.

DEVADATTA: Come, Padmini.

KAPILA: Go. But do you think I'll stay put while you run away with my wife? Where will you go? How far can you go? Only to the city, after all. I'll follow you there. I'll kick up a row in the streets. Let's see what happens then.

(*Devadatta stops.*)

PADMINI: Let him scream away. Don't pay him any attention.

DEVADATTA: No. He's right. This has to be solved here. It'll create a scandal in the city.

PADMINI: But who'll listen to him? Everyone will take you for Devadatta by your face.

KAPILA: Ha! You think the people in Dharmapura don't know my body, do you? They've seen me a thousand times in the wrestling pit. I've got I don't know how many awards for body-building. Let's see whom they believe.

PADMINI (*pleading*): Why are you tormenting us like this? For so many years you have been our friend, accepted our hospitality…

KAPILA: I know what you want, Padmini. Devadatta's clever head and Kapila's strong body…

PADMINI: Shut up, you brute.

DEVADATTA: Suppose she did. There's nothing wrong in it. It's natural for a woman to feel attracted to a fine figure of a man.

KAPILA: I know it is. But that doesn't mean she can just go and live with a man who's not her husband. That's not right.

PADMINI (*crying out*): How can we get rid of this scoundrel! Let's go—Let's go anywhere—to the woods—to the desert anywhere you like.

KAPILA: You'll have to kill me before you'll really escape me. You could. I don't have the strength to resist Kapila.

PADMINI (*using a new argument*): But I gave you life—

KAPILA: That was no favour. If you hadn't, you would have been a widow now. Actually he should be grateful to me because my wife saved his life. Instead, he's trying to snatch you away.

(*Padmini moans in agony.*)

DEVADATTA: This way we won't get anywhere, Kapila.

KAPILA: Call me Devadatta.

DEVADATTA: Whatever you are, this is no way to solve the problem.

KAPILA: Of course not. If marriage were a contract, it would be. But how can Padmini's fancy be taken as the solution?

DEVADATTA: Then what is the solution to this problem?

(*They all freeze.*)

BHAGAVATA: What? What indeed is the solution to this problem, which holds the entire future of these three unfortunate beings in a balance? Must their fate remain a mystery? And if so shall we not be insulting our audience by tying a question mark round its neck and bidding it good-bye? We have to face the problem. But it's a deep one and the answer must be sought with the greatest caution. Haste would be disastrous. So there's a break of ten minutes now. Please have some tea, ponder over this situation and come back with your own solutions. We shall then continue with our enquiry.

(*The stage-hands hold a white curtain in front of the frozen threesome, while the Bhagavata and others relax and sip tea.*)

ACT TWO

The white curtain is removed.

BHAGAVATA: What? What indeed is the solution to this problem, which holds the entire future of these three unfortunate beings in a balance?

Way back in the ages, when King Vikrama was ruling the world, shining in glory like the earth's challenge to the sun, he was asked the same question by the demon Vetala. And the king offered a solution even without, as it were, batting an eyelid. But will his rational, logical answer backed by the Sacred Texts appeal to our audience?

(*Sings.*)

The future pointed out by the tongue
safe inside the skull is not acceptable to us.
We must read the forehead which Brahma
has disconnected from the entrails.
We must unravel the net on the palm
disclaimed by the brain.
We must plumb the hidden depths of the
rivers running under our veins.

Yes, that would be the right thing to do.

So our three unfortunate friends went to a great *rishi* in search of a solution to their problem. And the *rishi*—remembering perhaps what King Vikrama had said—gave the verdict:

(*In a loud, sonorous voice.*)

As the heavenly Kalpa Vriksha is supreme among trees, so is the head among human limbs. Therefore the man with Devadatta's head is indeed Devadatta and he is the rightful husband of Padmini.

(*The three spring to life. Devadatta and Padmini scream with delight and move to one corner of the stage, laughing and dancing. Kapila, brokenhearted, drags his feet to the other corner.*)

DEVADATTA (*embracing Padmini*): My Padmini ... my lovely Padmini...
PADMINI: My King—My Master...
DEVADATTA: My little lightning...
PADMINI: The light of my joy...
DEVADATTA: The flower of my palm...
PADMINI: My celestial-bodied Gandharva ... My sun-faced Indra...
DEVADATTA: My Queen of Indra's Court...
PADMINI (*caressing his shoulders*): Come. Let's go. Let's go quickly. Where the earth is soft and the green grass plays the swing.
DEVADATTA: Let us. Where the banyan spreads a canopy and curtains off the skies.
PADMINI: What a wide chest. What other canopy do I need?
DEVADATTA: My soft, swaying Padmini. What other swing do I want?
PADMINI: My Devadatta comes like a bridegroom with the jewellery of a new body...
DEVADATTA (*a manly laugh*): And who should wear the jewellery but the eager bride?
PADMINI: Let's go. (*Pause.*) Wait. (*She runs to Kapila.*) Don't be sad, Kapila. We shall meet again, shan't we? (*In a low voice, so Devadatta can't hear.*) It's my duty to go with Devadatta. But remember I'm going with your body. Let that cheer you up. (*Goes back to Devadatta.*) Good-bye, Kapila.
DEVADATTA: Good-bye.
(*They go out, laughing, rubbing against each other. Kapila stands mute for a while. Then moves.*)
BHAGAVATA: Kapila—Kapila ... (*No reply.*) Don't grieve. It's fate, Kapila, and...
KAPILA: Kapila? What? Me? Why am I Kapila?
(*Exits.*)
BHAGAVATA: So the roads diverged. Kapila went into the forest and disappeared. He never saw Dharmapura again. In fact, he never felt the wind of any city again. As for Devadatta and Padmini, they returned to Dharmapura and plunged into the joys of married life.

(*Padmini enters and sits. She is stitching clothes, Devadatta comes. He is carrying in his hands two large dolls—which could be played by two children. The dolls are dressed in a way which makes it impossible to decide their sex.*

Devadatta comes in quietly and stands behind Padmini.)

DEVADATTA: Hey!

PADMINI (*startled*): Oh! Really, Devadatta. You startled me. The needle pricked me! Look, my finger's bleeding.

DEVADATTA: Tut—Tut! Is it really? Put it in my mouth. I'll suck it.

PADMINI: No, thanks. I'll suck it myself. (*Sees the dolls.*) How pretty! Whose are these?

DEVADATTA: Whose? Ours, of course! The guest is arriving soon. He must have playmates.

PADMINI: But the guest won't be coming for months yet, silly, and…

DEVADATTA: I know he isn't, but you can't get dolls like these any time you like! These are special dolls from the Ujjain fair.

PADMINI: They are lovely! (*Hugs the dolls.*) They look almost alive—such shining eyes—such delicate cheeks. (*Kisses them.*) Now sit down and tell me everything that happened at the fair. You wouldn't take me with you…

DEVADATTA: How could I—in your condition? I went only because you insisted you wanted to keep your word. But I'm glad I went. A very funny thing happened. There was a wrestling pit and a wrestler from Kamarupa was challenging people to fight him. I don't know what got into me. Before I'd even realized it, I had stripped and jumped into the pit.

PADMINI (*fondling the dolls*): You didn't! You've never ever wrestled before…

DEVADATTA: Didn't think of anything. I felt 'inspired'! Within a couple of minutes, I had pinned him to the ground.

PADMINI (*laughs out*): What would your father say if he heard of this?

DEVADATTA: My few acquaintances there were quite amazed.

PADMINI (*caressing his arm*): That day in the gymnasium you defeated the champion in a sword-fight. Now this! Don't overdo it: people may start suspecting.

DEVADATTA: Of course they won't. I was standing there bare-bodied and not a soul suspected. A friend even asked me if I'd learnt it from Kapila.

PADMINI: You have, after all!

(*They laugh.*)

DEVADATTA: You know, I'd always thought one had to use one's brains while wrestling or fencing or swimming. But this body just doesn't wait for thoughts—it acts!

PADMINI: Fabulous body—fabulous brain—fabulous Devadatta.

DEVADATTA: I have been running around all these days without even proper sleep and yet I don't feel a bit tired. (*Jumps up.*) Come on, we'll have a picnic by the lake. I feel like a good, long swim.

PADMINI (*mocking*): In my condition?

DEVADATTA: I didn't ask you to swim. You sit there and enjoy the scenery. Once our son's born, I'll teach you to swim too.

PADMINI: You go on about it being a son. What if it's a daughter?

DEVADATTA: If she's a daughter like you, I'll teach the two of you together.

PADMINI: Ready!

(*He pulls her to him.*)

Now—now—what about the picnic?

DEVADATTA: Quite right. First things first.

PADMINI (*pause*): Devadatta…

DEVADATTA: Yes?

PADMINI: Why do you—have to apply that sandal oil on your body?

DEVADATTA: I like it.

PADMINI: I know, but…

DEVADATTA: What?

PADMINI (*hesitating*): Your body had that strong, male smell before—I liked it.

DEVADATTA: But I've been using sandal oil since I was a child!

PADMINI: I don't mean that. But—when we came back from the temple of Kali—you used to smell so manly…

DEVADATTA: You mean that unwashed, sweaty smell Kapila had? (*Incredulous.*) You liked that?

PADMINI (*pause. Then lightly*): It was just a thought. Come on, let's start. We'll be late.

(*They go out. A long silence.*)

DOLL I: Not a bad house, I would say.

DOLL II: Could have been worse. I was a little worried.

DOLL I: This is the least we deserved. Actually we should have got a palace. A real palace!

DOLL II: And a prince to play with. A real prince!

DOLL I: How the children looked at us at the fair! How their eyes glowed!

DOLL II: How their mothers stared at us! How their mouths watered!

DOLL I: Only those beastly men turned up their noses! 'Expensive! Too expensive!'

DOLL II: Presuming to judge us! Who do they think they are!

DOLL I: Only a prince would be worthy of us.

DOLL II: We should be dusted every day…

DOLL I: … dressed in silk…

DOLL II: … seated on a cushioned shelf…

DOLL I: … given new clothes every week.

DOLL II: If the doll-maker had any sense, he'd never have sold us.

DOLL I: If he had any brains, he should never have given us to this man…

DOLL II: … with his rough labourer's hands.

DOLL I: Palms like wood…

DOLL II: A grip like a vice…

DOLL I: My arms are still aching.

DOLL II: He doesn't deserve us, the peasant.

(*Devadatta comes running in, tosses the dolls in the air, catches them and kisses them.*)

DEVADATTA: My dolls, your prince has arrived! The prince has come!

DOLL I (*in agony*): Brute! An absolute brute!

DOLL II (*in agony*): Beast! A complete beast!

DEVADATTA (*runs to the Bhagavata*): Here, Bhagavata Sir, take these sweets. You must come to the feast tomorrow at our house.

BHAGAVATA: What's it for?

DEVADATTA: Haven't you heard? I've got a son like a gem—a son like a rose—Yippeee…

(*He goes out dancing some* Lezim *steps. A long silence.*)

DOLL I: Is that little satan asleep yet?

DOLL II: Think so. God! It's killing me…

DOLL I: … crying, all day…

DOLL II: … making a mess every fifteen minutes.

DOLL I: What have we come to! One should never trust God.

DOLL II: It's our fault. We should have been wary from the moment we saw that child in her dreams.

DOLL I: We should have noticed she was bloating day by day.

DOLL II: We should have suspected foul play then.

DOLL I: It wasn't our fault. How could we know she was hiding this thing inside her?

DOLL II: How she was swelling! Day by day! Week by week! As though someone were blowing air into her…

DOLL I: How ugly she looked…

DOLL II: … not to her husband, though!

DOLL I: When they were alone, he would place his hand on her belly and say, 'Is he kicking now?'

DOLL II (*seriously*): We should have been on our guard.

DOLL I (*dispirited*): We should.

DOLL II: And then comes this little monster.

DOLL I: … this lump of flesh…

DOLL II: It doesn't even have proper eyes or ears…

DOLL I: … but it gets all the attention.

DOLL II (*in disgust*): Ugh…

DOLL I (*sick*): Awk…

(*Devadatta and Padmini enter with the child, for which a wooden doll may be used. They walk across the stage, engrossed in talking to and about the child, and go out.*)

DOLL I: A spider's built its web around my shoulders.
DOLL II: Yesterday a mouse nibbled at my toe.
DOLL I: The other day a cockroach ate my left eye.
DOLL II: Six months—and not a soul has come near us.
DOLL I: Six months—and not a hand has touched us.
DOLL II: Six months and we reach this state. What'll happen in a year's time?
(*Padmini and Devadatta enter.*)
PADMINI: Listen.
DEVADATTA: Yes.
PADMINI: You mustn't say 'no'—at least this time.
DEVADATTA: To what?
PADMINI: We'll take him to the lake.
DEVADATTA: In this cold?
PADMINI: What if it's cold? He's older now. There's no need to mollycoddle him. I grew up running around in heat and cold and rain—and nothing happened to me. I'm all right.
DEVADATTA: No, it's unnecessary trouble for everyone.
PADMINI: What do you mean trouble? What's happened to you these days? You sit at home all day. Never go out. You've forgotten all your swimming and sports.
DEVADATTA: I'm a Brahmin, Padmini. My duty…
PADMINI: I've heard all this!
DEVADATTA: It was fun the first few days because it was new. All that muscle and strength. But how long can one go on like that? I have a family tradition to maintain—the daily reading, writing and studies…
PADMINI: I don't know.
DEVADATTA (*affectionate*): Now look here, Padmini…
(*Puts his hand round her shoulder. She suddenly shudders.*)
Why? What happened?
PADMINI: Nothing—I don't know why—I suddenly had goose flesh.
(*Pause.*)
DEVADATTA (*withdrawing his hand*): Do you know where I've kept the copy of *Dharma Sindhu*? I've been looking for it.

PADMINI: I think I saw it on the shelf. Must be there…

(*Devadatta goes to Doll I, moves it aside and picks up the book. Doll I shudders.*)

DOLL II: Why? What happened?

DOLL I: He touched me, and…

DOLL II: Yes?

DOLL I: His palms! They were so rough once, when he first brought us here. Like a labourer's. But now they are soft—sickly soft—like a young girl's.

DOLL II: I know. I've noticed something too.

DOLL I: What?

DOLL II: His stomach. It was so tight and muscular. Now…

DOLL I: I know. It's soft and loose.

DOLL II: Do you think it'll swell up too?

(*They laugh.*)

DOLL I (*holding its hands in front of its stomach to suggest a swollen belly*): It'll swell a little…

DOLL II (*holding its hands a little farther in front*): —then more…

DOLL I (*even further*): —more and…

DOLL II (*even further*): —and more until…

DOLL I: … if it's a woman…

DOLL II: … there'll be a child…

DOLL I: … and if it's a man…

DOLL II: BANG!

(*They roll with laughter. Padmini comes in with the child. She sings a lullaby.*)

PADMINI: Here comes a rider!
From what land does he come?
On his head a turban
with a long pearly tail.
Round his neck a garland
of virgin-white jasmines.
In his fist a sword
with a diamond-studded hilt.
The white-clad rider

rides a white charger
which spreads its tossing mane
against the western sky,
spreads its mane like breakers
against the western sky.
Sleep now, my baby
and see smiling dreams.
There he comes—here he is!
From which land does he come?
But why are the jasmines on his chest
red O so red?
What shine in his open eyes?
Pebbles O pebbles.
Why is his young body
cold O so cold?
The white horse gallops
across hills, streams and fields.
To what land does he gallop?
Nowhere O nowhere.

(*Half-way through the lullaby, Devadatta comes in and sits by Padmini's side, reading. They don't look at each other. At the end of the lullaby, they fall asleep.*)

DOLL I (*in a hushed voice*): Hey.

DOLL II: Yes?

DOLL I: Look.

DOLL II: Where?

DOLL I: Behind her eyelids. She is dreaming.

DOLL II: I don't see anything.

DOLL I: It's still hazy—hasn't started yet. Do you see it now?

DOLL II (*eagerly*): Yes, yes.

(*They stare at her.*)

DOLL I: A man.

DOLL II: But not her husband.

DOLL I: No, someone else.

DOLL II: Is this the one who came last night?

DOLL I: Yes—the same. But I couldn't see his face then.

DOLL II: You can now. Not very nice—rough. Like a labourer's. But he's got a nice body—looks soft.

DOLL I: Who do you think it is?

DOLL II: I—It's fading. (*Urgently.*) Remember the face!

DOLL I: It's fading—Oh! It's gone!

DOLL II: And she won't even remember it tomorrow.

(*Padmini and Devadatta sit up.*)

PADMINI: Are you ill?

DEVADATTA: Why?

PADMINI: You were moaning in your sleep last night.

DEVADATTA: Was I?

PADMINI: Aren't you feeling well?

DEVADATTA: Who? Me? I'm fine.

(*Gets up energetically to show how well he feels. Suddenly grabs his shoulder with a groan.*)

PADMINI: What's wrong? Tell me.

DEVADATTA (*avoiding her eyes*): Nothing. I went to the gymnasium yesterday morning. Then went swimming.

PADMINI: To the gymnasium? After all these years? But why?

DEVADATTA: I just felt like it. That's all. Don't go on about it.

PADMINI (*without irony*): Are you going again today?

DEVADATTA (*flares up*): No, I'm not. And there's no need to laugh. I know I've made a fool of myself by going there. I won't again.

(*Goes out. Long pause.*)

PADMINI: What are you afraid of, Devadatta? What does it matter that you are going soft again, that you are losing your muscles? I'm not going to be stupid again. Kapila's gone out of my life—forever. I won't let him come back again. (*Pause.*) Kapila? What could he be doing now? Where could he be? Could his body be fair still, and his face dark? (*Long pause.*) Devadatta changes. Kapila changes. And me?

(*Closes her eyes.*)

DOLL I: There he is again.

DOLL II: In the middle of the day?

DOLL I (*doubtful*): I'm not sure this is the usual visitor. This one looks rougher and darker.

DOLL II: It's him all right. Look at his face.

DOLL I: He goes to her...

DOLL II: ... very near her...

DOLL I (*in a whisper*): What's he going to do now?

DOLL II (*even more anxious*): What?

(*They watch.*)

DOLL I (*baffled*): But he's climbing a tree!

DOLL II (*almost a wail of disappointment*): He's dived into a river!

DOLL I: Is that all he came for?

DOLL II: It's going...

DOLL I: ... going...

DOLL II: Gone! Wretched dreams! They just tickle and fade away.

(*Padmini wakes up and mimes putting the crying child to sleep.*)

PADMINI (*suddenly vicious*): Change! Change! Change! Change! Change! The sand trickles. The water fills the pot. And the moon goes on swinging, swinging, swinging, from light to darkness to light.

(*Devadatta comes in. He is now completely changed to his original self.*)

DEVADATTA: A pundit's coming to see me. He wants me to explain some verses to him. Can you keep some sweets and lime-juice ready?

PADMINI: Yes. (*Pause.*) Did you hear...? The maid was telling me.

DEVADATTA: What?

PADMINI: Kapila's mother died this morning. (*Pause.*) Poor thing! She'd been bed-ridden all these years, ever since...

DEVADATTA (*snapping at her*): What did you expect me to do about it? (*Then embarrassed.*) Get the lime-juice ready soon.

(*They go out.*)

DOLL I: Each one to his fate!

DOLL II: Each one to her problems!

DOLL I: As the doll-maker used to say, 'What are things coming to!'

DOLL II: Especially last night—I mean—that dream...

DOLL I: Tut! Tut! One shouldn't talk about such things!

DOLL II: It was so shameless…
DOLL I: I said be quiet…
DOLL II: Honestly! The way they…
DOLL I: Look, if we must talk about it, let me tell.
DOLL II: You don't want to talk about it. So.
DOLL I: You don't understand a thing. They…
DOLL II: What do you know? Last night…
DOLL I: Let me! In that dream…
DOLL II: I'm…
DOLL I: Shut up!
DOLL II: You shut up!

(*They start arguing, then fighting. They roll on the ground, on top of each other, biting, scratching, hitting each other. They shout, scream and giggle. As they fight, the giggles become louder and more frantic. Their clothes get torn. At last they lie side by side panting, bursting with little giggles. Then they sit up. Padmini enters, looks at them.*)

PADMINI: Just look at the dolls! The baby's really torn them to rags. How long can we go on with them! (*Calls.*) Listen.
DEVADATTA (*entering*): Yes.
PADMINI: We must get new dolls for our baby. These are in tatters.
DEVADATTA: You're right. I hadn't noticed.
PADMINI: The Ujjain fair is to be held in another four days. Why don't you go and get new dolls there? If you start today you'll be there in time for it. It's unlucky to keep torn dolls at home.
DOLL I (*to Doll II*): Did you hear that? She wants to throw us out…
DOLL II: She wants new dolls.
DOLL I: The whore.
DOLL II: The bitch.
DOLL I: May her house burn down.
DOLL II: May her teeth fall out.
DEVADATTA (*to Padmini*): All right.

(*He picks them up by their collars.*)

DOLL I: See how he picks us up. Like stray puppies.
DOLL II: That ball of flesh will remain here. But it's the dung-heap for us.

DEVADATTA (*to Padmini*): It'll take me more than a week to go to Ujjain and come back. Shall I ask one of the neighbours to get them for us?

DOLL I (*to Devadatta*): You wretch—before you throw us out watch out for yourself.

DOLL II: Cover your wife before you start worrying about our rags.

PADMINI (*to Devadatta*): Who knows what sort of dolls they'll get for us? We must bring things ourselves for our baby.

DEVADATTA: But...

PADMINI: If you don't want to go, say so. Don't...

DEVADATTA: Shall I ask one of the servants to come and sleep here at night while I'm away?

PADMINI: No need. We are not in the middle of a forest.

DOLL I (*to Devadatta*): Watch out, you fool...

DOLL II: Refuse, you idiot...

DEVADATTA: All right. I'll start at once. Take care of yourself.

(*He drags the dolls out.*)

DOLL I: Villain...

DOLL II: Rascal...

DOLL I: Swine...

DOLL II: Bastard...

(*One can hear them screaming curses as he takes them out. Padmini stands watching him go. Then to the child in her arms.*)

PADMINI: My poor child, you haven't yet seen the witching fair of the dark forest, have you? Let's go and see it. How can I describe it to you? There's so much. Long before the sun rises, the shadows of twigs draw *alpanas* on the floor. The stars raise *arati* and go. Then the day dawns and the fun begins. The circus in the tree-tops and the cock-fights in a shower of feathers. And the dances! The tiger-dance, and the peacock-dance, and the dance of the sun's little feet with silver anklets on the river. In the heart of the forest stands the stately chariot of the shield-bearer. It's made of pure gold—rows of egrets pull it down the street, and rows of flames of the forest salute it with torches. Then the night comes, and our poor baby is tired. So we blow gently and out goes the moon. But before we leave, there's one more thing to do. Right outside the fair, watching it from a distance, stands the tree of the Fortunate Lady. It's an old tree, a close friend of ours. We have to say 'hello' to it. All right?

(*She goes out with the child. A long silence. Kapila enters. He too is as he was at the beginning of the play, tough and muscular.*)

BHAGAVATA: Who? Kapila?

KAPILA: Yes.

BHAGAVATA: It's such a long time since we met.

KAPILA: Yes.

BHAGAVATA: Where are you now?

KAPILA: Here.

BHAGAVATA: Here? In this jungle! It's difficult to believe any man could live here.

KAPILA: Beasts do. Why not men?

BHAGAVATA: What do you do?

KAPILA: Live.

BHAGAVATA: Have you had any news from the city?

KAPILA: Long ago. Father sent word asking me to come back. I said, 'I won't come. No need for you to come here either!' That's all.

BHAGAVATA: You mean—you don't know your father died last year? Also your mother…

KAPILA (*expressionless*): No.

BHAGAVATA: And Padmini has a son.

KAPILA: I see.

BHAGAVATA: Why this anger, Kapila?

KAPILA: What anger?

BHAGAVATA: It shows in the way you stand, you move.

KAPILA: All that is your poetry.

(*Moves on.*)

BHAGAVATA: Kapila! Kapila!

(*Kapila goes round the stage once. He mimes picking up an axe and felling a tree. A long silence. Only the soundless image of Kapila cutting the tree.*

Padmini enters, child in arms. She is scared and walks in rapidly. She sees Kapila and stands transfixed. Kapila doesn't see her for a while and when he does, stands paralysed. A long silence.)

KAPILA (*slowly*): You?

PADMINI: Yes.

KAPILA: Here?

PADMINI: My son had never laughed with the river or shivered in the wind or felt the thorn cut his feet. So I brought him out. I lost my way in the woods.

KAPILA: You shouldn't have lost it this far.

PADMINI: The wrong road stuck to my feet; wouldn't let go.

KAPILA: You shouldn't have lost it this far. Wild beasts—robbers—pathless paths—all sorts of dangers.

PADMINI: I asked the villagers. And the pilgrims. And the hunters. And the tribesmen. When there wasn't anyone any more, I asked myself. Everyone saw to it that I didn't lose the wrong road.

(*Pause.*)

KAPILA: Is that your son?

PADMINI: Yes. And yours.

KAPILA: Mine?

PADMINI: Your body gave him to me.

KAPILA: Mine? (*Erupting.*) Not mine. I'm Kapila, Padmini. I didn't accept it that day. But I accept it now, I'm Kapila.

PADMINI (*softly*): And how's Kapila?

(*The Bhagavata sings. The following is a prose rendering of the song.*)

BHAGAVATA: Once I spread my wings, and kicked away the earth and flew up. I covered the seven continents, the ten shores and measured the sky.

Now because you have a child at your breast, a husband on your thighs, the red of rust on the lips of your late-opening mouth, I pick a picture here, and there a card of fate, and live for the grace of a grain—an astrologer's bird.

KAPILA: Can I look at him?

PADMINI: That's why I brought him.

(*Kapila looks at the child.*)

KAPILA: What's wrong with me? You've come so far and I haven't even asked you to sit down. Why don't you go in and take a little rest?

(*She goes in with the child. He stands as in a daze. She comes out without the child.*)

KAPILA: Why...

PADMINI: I don't need any rest.

(*Long silence.*)

KAPILA: How are you?

PADMINI: I'm well. No illness, problems or difficulties.

KAPILA: Your son looks exactly like you.

PADMINI (*a slight pause*): And you.

(*Kapila doesn't reply.*)

He has the same mole on his shoulder.

KAPILA: What mole?

(*She comes to him and points out the mole on his shoulder.*)

PADMINI: This one. Which other could it be? That's the only one you have on your shoulder.

KAPILA: Oh! I hadn't seen it. I don't much look at this body.

PADMINI (*quietly*): Do you despise it that much?

(*No reply.*)

Why have you tortured it so?

(*Takes his hand in hers.*)

When this went to you, it was so soft, like a prince's. These arms were so slender and fair. Look at them now. Why have you done this to yourself?

KAPILA: When this body came to me, it was like a corpse hanging by my head. It was a Brahmin's body after all: not made for the woods. I couldn't lift an axe without my elbows moaning. Couldn't run a length without my knees howling. I had no use for it. The moment it came to me, a war started between us.

PADMINI: And who won?

KAPILA: I did.

PADMINI: The head always wins, doesn't it?

KAPILA: Fortunately, yes. Now I can run ten miles and not stop for breath. I can swim through the monsoon floods and fell a banyan.

The stomach used to rebel once. Now it digests what I give. If I don't, it doesn't complain.

PADMINI: Must the head always win?

KAPILA: That's why I am Kapila now. Kapila! Kapila with a body which fits his face.

PADMINI: What a good mix
No more tricks
Is this one that
Or that one this?

Do you remember the song we sang in the Kali temple?

KAPILA: So?

PADMINI: Nothing. I often remember it. It's almost my autobiography now. Kapila! Devadatta! Kapila with Devadatta's body! Devadatta with Kapila's body! Four men in a single lifetime.

KAPILA (*suddenly*): Why have you come away from him?

PADMINI: What do you want me to say?

(*They freeze.*)

BHAGAVATA: How could I make you understand? If Devadatta had changed overnight and had gone back to his original form, I would have forgotten you completely. But that's not how it happened. He changed day by day. Inch by inch. Hair by hair. Like the trickling sand. Like the water filling the pot. And as I saw him change, I couldn't get rid of you. That's what Padmini must tell Kapila. She should say more, without concealing anything. 'Kapila, if that *rishi* had given me to you, would I have gone back to Devadatta some day exactly like this?' But she doesn't say anything. She remains silent.

KAPILA (*to Padmini*): Why have you come here?

PADMINI: I had to see you.

KAPILA: Why? (*No reply.*) Why? Why did you have to come just when I thought I'd won this long and weary battle? Why did you have to pursue me just when I had succeeded in uprooting these memories? I am Kapila now. The rough and violent Kapila. Kapila without a crack between his head and his shoulders. What do you want now? Another head? Another suicide? Listen to me. Do me a favour. Go back. Back to Devadatta. He is your husband, the father of this child. Devadatta and Padmini! Devadatta and Padmini! A pair coupled with the holy fire as the witness. I have no place there, no peace, no salvation. So go. I beg of you. Go.

(*A long silence.*)

PADMINI: I will. If you want me to.

KAPILA (*almost a moan*): Oh God!

PADMINI: Why?

KAPILA: Nothing. Another memory—when I too was asked to go—Yes, go back. Now.

PADMINI: I will. But can I ask a little favour? My son's tired. He's asleep. He has been in my arms for several days now. Let him rest a while. As soon as he gets up I'll go. (*Laughs.*) Yes, you won, Kapila. Devadatta won too. But I—the better half of two bodies—I neither win nor lose. No, don't say anything. I know what you'll say and I've told myself that a thousand times. It's my fault. I mixed the heads up. I must suffer the consequences. I will. I'm sorry I came. I didn't think before I started. Couldn't. But at least until my child wakes up, may I sit here and look at you? Have my fill for the rest of my life? I won't speak a word.

(*Long pause.*)

KAPILA: What does it matter now whether you stay or go? You've done the damage. I had buried all those faceless memories in my skin. Now you've dug them up with your claws.

PADMINI: Why should one bury anything?

KAPILA: Why shouldn't one? Why should one tolerate this mad dance of incompleteness?

PADMINI: Whose incompleteness? Yours?

KAPILA: Yes, mine. One beats the body into shape, but one can't beat away the memories trapped in it. Isn't that surprising? That the body should have its own ghosts, its own secrets? Memories of touch—memories of *a* touch—memories of a body swaying in these arms, of a warm skin against this palm—memories which one cannot recognize, cannot understand, cannot even name because this head wasn't there when they happened.

PADMINI: Kapila...

KAPILA (*without anger*): Why did you come? You came. You touched me. You held my hand, and my body recognized your touch. I have never touched you, but this body, this appendage, laughed and flowered out in a festival of memories to which I'm an outcaste.

PADMINI: Poor Kapila!

KAPILA: Don't pity me.

PADMINI: Be quiet, stupid. Your body bathed in a river, swam and danced in it. Shouldn't your head know what river it was, what swim? Your head too must submerge in that river: the flow must rumple your hair, run its tongue in your ears and press your head to its bosom. Until that's done, you'll continue to be incomplete.

(*Kapila raises his head and looks at her. She caresses his face, like a blind person trying to imprint it on her finger-tips. Then she rests her head on his chest.*)

My Kapila! My poor, poor Kapila! How needlessly you've tortured yourself.

(*Kapila lifts her up and takes her in.*)

BHAGAVATA: You cannot engrave on water
nor wound it with a knife,
which is why
the river
has no fear
of memories.

FEMALE CHORUS: The river only feels the
pull of the waterfall.
She giggles, and tickles the rushes
on the bank, then turns
a top of dry leaves
in the navel of the whirlpool, weaves
a water-snake in the net of silver strands
in its green depths, frightens the frog
on the rug of moss, sticks and bamboo leaves,
sings, tosses, leaps and
sweeps on in a rush—

BHAGAVATA: While the scarecrow on the bank
has a face fading
on its mudpot head
and a body torn
with memories.

(*Devadatta enters. He is holding a sword in one hand, and in the other, two dolls, made of cloth.*)

BHAGAVATA: Who! Devadatta?

DEVADATTA: Where does Kapila live here?

BHAGAVATA: Uhm—well—Anyway, how are … you…

DEVADATTA: If you don't want to tell me, don't. I can find out for myself.

BHAGAVATA: There. Behind those trees.

DEVADATTA: How long has Padmini been here?

BHAGAVATA: About four or five days.

DEVADATTA: Amazing! Even a man like me found the road hard. But how quickly she covered it—and with a child in her arms.

BHAGAVATA: Devadatta…

(*Devadatta moves on.*)

Devadatta moves on. There are only two words which make sense to him now—Kapila and Padmini! Kapila and Padmini! The words sweep him along to the doorstep of Kapila's hut. But suddenly he stops. Until this moment he has been rearing to taste the blood of Kapila. But now he is still and calm.

(*Kapila comes out.*)

KAPILA: Come, Devadatta. I was waiting for you. I've been expecting you since yesterday. I have been coming out every half an hour to see if you'd arrived. Not from fear. Only eager.

(*Padmini comes out and stands watching them.*)

KAPILA (*to Devadatta*): You look exactly the same.

DEVADATTA (*laughs*): You too.

KAPILA (*points to the sword*): What's that?

DEVADATTA (*extending the hand which holds the dolls*): Dolls. For the child. I came home from the fair. There was no one there. So I came here.

(*Padmini steps forward and takes the dolls. But neither speaks. Padmini goes back to her place and stands clutching the dolls to her bosom.*)

KAPILA: Come in and rest a while. There'll always be time to talk later.

(*Devadatta shakes his head.*)

Why? Are you angry?

DEVADATTA: Not any more. (*Pause.*) Did my body bother you too much?

KAPILA: It wasn't made for this life. It resisted. It also had its revenge.

DEVADATTA: Did it?

KAPILA: Do you remember how I once used to envy you your poetry, your ability to imagine things? For me, the sky was the sky, and the tree only a tree. Your body gave me new feelings, new words. I felt awake as I'd never before. Even started writing poems. Very bad ones, I'm afraid.

(*They laugh.*)

There were times when I hated it for what it gave me.

DEVADATTA: I wanted your power but not your wildness. You lived in hate—I in fear.

KAPILA: No, I was the one who was afraid.

DEVADATTA: What a good mix. No more tricks.

(*They laugh.*)

Tell me one thing. Do you really love Padmini?

KAPILA: Yes.

DEVADATTA: So do I.

KAPILA: I know.

(*Silence.*)

Devadatta, couldn't we all three live together—like the Pandavas and Draupadi?

DEVADATTA: What do you think?

(*Silence. Padmini looks at them but doesn't say anything.*)

KAPILA (*laughs*): No, it can't be done.

DEVADATTA: That's why I brought this. (*Shows the sword.*) What won't end has to be cut.

KAPILA: I got your body, but not your wisdom.

DEVADATTA: Where's your sword then?

KAPILA: A moment.

(*Goes in. Padmini stands looking at Devadatta. But he looks somewhere far away.*)

BHAGAVATA: After sharing with Indra
his wine
his food
his jokes
I returned to the earth
and saw from far—
a crack had appeared
in the earth's face—
exactly
like Indra's smile

(*Kapila returns with his sword. They take up positions.*)

KAPILA: Are you still in practice?

DEVADATTA: Of course not. But you'd learned well. And you?

KAPILA: I learnt again. But one's older now—slower at learning.

DEVADATTA (*pause*): You realize it's immaterial who's better with a sword now, don't you?

KAPILA: Yes, I do.

DEVADATTA: There's only one solution to this.

KAPILA: We must both die.

DEVADATTA: We must both die.

KAPILA: With what confidence we chopped off our heads in that temple! Now whose head—whose body—suicide or murder—nothing's clear.

DEVADATTA: No grounds for friendship now. No question of mercy. We must fight like lions and kill like cobras.

KAPILA: Let our heads roll to the very hands which cut them in the temple of Kali!

(*Music starts. The fight is stylized like a dance. Their swords don't touch. Even Padmini's reaction is like a dance.*)

BHAGAVATA (*sings*): Like cocks in a pit
we dance—he and I,

foot woven with foot
eye soldered to eye.
He knows and I know
all there's to be known:
the witch's burning thirst
burns for blood alone.
Hence this frozen smile,
which cracks and drips to earth,
and claw-knives, digging flesh
for piecemeal death.

The *rishi* who said 'Knowledge gives rise to forgiveness' had no knowledge of death.

(*Kapila wounds Devadatta who falls to his feet and fights. He stabs Kapila. Both fight on their knees, fall and die.*
A long silence. Padmini slowly comes and sits between the bodies.)

PADMINI: They burned, lived, fought, embraced and died. I stood silent. If I'd said, 'Yes, I'll live with you both', perhaps they would have been alive yet. But I couldn't say it. I couldn't say, 'Yes'. No, Kapila, no, Devadatta. I know it in my blood you couldn't have lived together. You would've had to share not only me but your bodies as well. Because you knew death you died in each other's arms. You could only have lived ripping each other to pieces. I had to drive you to death. You forgave each other, but again, left me out.

BHAGAVATA (*without leaving his seat*): What is this? It's a sight to freeze the blood in one's veins. What happened, child? Can we help you?

PADMINI (*without looking at him*): Yes, please. My son is sleeping in the hut. Take him under your care. Give him to the hunters who live in this forest and tell them it's Kapila's son. They loved Kapila and will bring the child up. Let the child grow up in the forest with the rivers and the trees. When he's five take him to the Revered Brahmin Vidyasagara of Dharmapura. Tell him it's Devadatta's son.

BHAGAVATA: And you?

PADMINI: Make me a large funeral pyre. We are three.

BHAGAVATA: You mean you are performing *sati*? But why, child?

PADMINI (*puts the dolls on the ground*): Give these dolls to my son. I won't see him. He may tempt me away from my path.

(*At a sign from the Bhagavata, two stage-hands come and place a curtain in front of Padmini.*)

Kali, Mother of all Nature, you must have your joke even now. Other women can die praying that they should get the same husband in all the lives to come. You haven't left me even that little consolation.

(*Does* namaskara. *The stage-hands lift the curtain, slowly, very slowly, very slowly, as the song goes on. The curtain has a blazing fire painted on it. And as it is lifted, the flames seem to leap up. The female musicians sing a song. The following is a prose rendering of it.*)

FEMALE CHORUS (*sings*): Our sister is leaving in a palanquin of sandalwood. Her mattress is studded with rubies which burn and glow. She is decked in flowers which blossom on tinder-wood and whose petals are made of molten gold. How the garlands leap and cover her, aflame with love.

The Fortunate Lady's procession goes up the street of laburnums, while the *makarandas* tie the pennants and the jacarandas hold the lights.

Good-bye, dear sister. Go you without fear. The Lord of Death will be pleased with the offering of three coconuts.

BHAGAVATA (*picks up the dolls and comes downstage*): Thus Padmini became a *sati*. India is known for its *pativratas*, wives who dedicated their whole existence to the service of their husbands; but it would not be an exaggeration to say that no *pativrata* went in the way Padmini did. And yet no one knows the spot where she performed *sati*. If you ask the hunting tribes who dwell in these forests, they only point to a full-blossomed tree of the Fortunate Lady. They say that even now on full moon and on new moon nights, a song rises from the roots of the tree and fills the whole forest like a fragrance.

FEMALE CHORUS (*sings*): Why should love stick to the sap of a single body? When the stem is drunk with the thick yearning of the many-petalled, many-flowered lantana, why should it be tied down to the relation of a single flower?

A head for each breast. A pupil for each eye. A side for each arm. I have neither regret nor shame. The blood pours into the earth and a song branches out in the sky.

(*When the song ends, the Bhagavata does a* namaskara *to the audience. The audience should get a definite feeling that the play has ended when a scream is heard in the wings.*)

BHAGAVATA: What's that? Oh! Nata, our Actor!

(*Actor II comes rushing out. He doesn't even see the Bhagavata in his desperate hurry.*)

Why is he running? Where's the National Anthem?

(*Actor II suddenly stops in his tracks.*)

ACTOR II: The National Anthem!

BHAGAVATA: What?

ACTOR II: How did you know?

BHAGAVATA: Know what?

ACTOR II: Please, Bhagavata Sir, how did you know...

BHAGAVATA: Know what?

ACTOR II: About the National Anthem.

BHAGAVATA: What do you mean?

ACTOR II: Please, Sir, I beg of you. I implore you. Don't make fun of me. How did you know it was the National Anthem...

BHAGAVATA: Why? Haven't you seen an audience...

ACTOR II (*relieved*): Phew! That! Ram Ram!

BHAGAVATA: Why? What happened?

ACTOR II: What happened? Sree Hari! Look...

(*Lifts his hand. It's trembling.*)

BHAGAVATA: Why? What...

ACTOR II: I almost died of fright...

BHAGAVATA: Really?

ACTOR II: I was coming down the road, when I heard someone singing at a distance, at the top of his voice. He was singing, *Jhanda*

Ooncha Rahe Hamara (May our flag fly high!) Then he proceeded to *Sare Jahan se Acchha Hindostan Hamara* (Our India is better than the whole world). Then *Rise, Rise my Kannada Land.* Then *Vande Mataram*...

BHAGAVATA: Then?

ACTOR II: I was baffled. A true patriot at this time of the night? I had to find out who it was. A house—a big, thick fence around with not a gap in it. But I managed to find a hole to crawl through. I was just half-way in when I saw...

BHAGAVATA: What?

(*The Actor wipes his brow.*)

Come on, what did you see?

ACTOR II: A horse!

BHAGAVATA (*eager*): A horse?

ACTOR II: Yes. It turned to me and in a deep, sonorous voice said, 'Friend, I'm now going to sing the National Anthem. So please do stand up to attention!'

BHAGAVATA: Listen, Nata, are you sure...

ACTOR II: I swear...

BHAGAVATA: No, no, what I mean is...

(*Commotion in the wings.*)

What's that now?

(*Actor I enters with a boy of about five. The boy is very serious, even sulky. There's not a trace of laughter on his face. He is holding the two cloth dolls which we have already seen, but the dolls are dirtier now. The commotion comes from Actor I, who is so busy trying to make the child laugh—making faces at him, clowning, capering, and shouting—he doesn't notice the Bhagavata.*)

BHAGAVATA (*delighted*): Oh! Nata! You again!

ACTOR I (*turns around and sees the Bhagavata*): Oh, Sir, it's you!

BHAGAVATA: Well well, you'll live to be a hundred.

ACTOR I: Why? What have I done?

BHAGAVATA: I was just thinking of you and you turned up. Just now this Nata (*pointing to Actor II*) was saying he saw a horse-headed man and I wondered if it was Hayavadana. So I remembered you.

ACTOR II: Bhagavata Sir...

ACTOR I (*ignoring Actor II*): There's an actor's fate in a nutshell for you. Always remembered for someone else.

BHAGAVATA: Where's Hayavadana now? Has he come back?

ACTOR I: I don't know, Sir. He chased me away the moment we reached the Kali temple. Wouldn't let me stay there a minute longer.

BHAGAVATA: Oh! I very much hope the goddess granted him what he wanted. (*Sees the child.*) Who's this child?

ACTOR I: Him? Well? (*To the child.*) Go on, tell him.

(*The child remains silent. Doesn't answer any questions.*)

BHAGAVATA: Who are you, child? What's your name? Where are your parents?

ACTOR I: You see? Not a word. Children of his age should be outtalking a dictionary, but this one doesn't speak a word. Doesn't laugh, doesn't cry, doesn't even smile. The same long face all twenty-four hours. There's obviously something wrong with him.

(*Bends before the child and clowns a bit.*)

See? No response—no reactions. When he grows up, he should make a good theatre critic.

ACTOR II (*restless*): Bhagavata Sir...

BHAGAVATA (*to Actor I*): Where did you find him?

ACTOR I: In a tribal village of hunters. On my way back I had to stay a night there and a tribal woman brought him to me. Said, 'This is not our child. It's from the city. Take it back'.

BHAGAVATA: A child of this city? (*Actor I nods.*) How strange! (*Notices the dolls.*) But—but—these dolls...

(*Tries to touch the dolls. The child reacts violently and moves away angry, terrified.*)

ACTOR I: I was about to warn you! Whatever you do, don't touch his dolls! At other times he'll starve and freeze to death rather than say a word. But touch the dolls and he'll bare his fangs. He almost bit off my finger once.

ACTOR II: Bhagavata Sir...

BHAGAVATA (*to Actor I*): But Nata—(*Pause.*) Child, let me see your shoulder.

(*The child moves back.*)

No, no, I won't touch the dolls. I promise you. Just your shoulder.

(*Inspects his shoulder. Then with a cry of triumph.*) Nata...

ACTOR II: Bhagavata Sir...

ACTOR I: Yes...

BHAGAVATA: Look, the mole. It's Padmini's son... There's no doubt about it.

ACTOR I: Padmini? Which...

ACTOR II (*shouting at the top of his voice*): Bhagavata Sir!

(*Actor I and the Bhagavata react.*)

BHAGAVATA: Yes? Why are you shouting?

ACTOR II: I have been calling you for the last half-an-hour...

BHAGAVATA: Yes, yes. What's it?

ACTOR II: You said I'd seen a horse-headed man. I didn't. What I saw was a complete, perfect, proper...

(*A voice is heard off-stage singing the third stanza of 'Jana Gana Mana'.*)

There it is!

(*All stare in the direction of the song. A horse enters the stage singing.*)

HORSE: *Tava Karunaruna Rage*
Nidrita Bharata Jage
Tava Charane Nata Matha
Jaya Jaya Jaya He Jaya Rajeshwara

(*Comes and stands in front of them.*)

Hohoo! What's this? Mr Bhagavata Sir! My Actor friend! Well, well, well! What a pleasant surprise! Delightful! How are you, Sir, how are you?

BHAGAVATA: It's not—not Hayavadana, is it?

HAYAVADANA: Your most obedient servant, Sir.

BHAGAVATA: But what...

ACTOR II: You mean you know this horse?

BHAGAVATA (*bursts into a guffaw*): We're old friends.

ACTOR I (*laughing*): Fellow-pilgrims!

HAYAVADANA: But not fellow-travellers. What?

(*They roar with laughter. Suddenly the boy too starts laughing. Doubles up with laughter. The dolls fall out of his hand as he claps his hands.*)

THE BOY (*clapping his hands*): The horse is laughing! The horse is laughing!

ACTOR I (*jumping with delight*): The boy is laughing!

HAYAVADANA (*goes to the boy*): Why, my little friend, you may laugh, but I may not?

(*The boy is in hysterics.*)

DEVADATTA: That's Padmini's son, Hayavadana.

HAYAVADANA: Padmini? I am not aware of…

BHAGAVATA: You don't know her. But this poor child—he hadn't laughed, or cried, or talked in all these years. Now you have made him laugh.

HAYAVADANA: Delighted. Delighted.

BHAGAVATA: But tell me: you went to the goddess to become a complete man, didn't you? What happened?

HAYAVADANA: Ah! That's a long story. I went there, picked up a sword which was lying around—very unsafe, I tell you—put it on my neck and said: 'Mother of all Nature, if you don't help me, I'll chop off my head!'

ACTOR I: Then?

HAYAVADANA: The goddess appeared. Very prompt. But looked rather put out. She said—rather peevishly, I thought—'Why don't you people go somewhere else if you want to chop off your stupid heads? Why do you have to come to me?' I fell at her feet and said, 'Mother, make me complete'. She said 'So be it' and disappeared—even before I could say 'Make me a complete man!' I became a horse.

ACTOR I: I am sorry to hear that…

HAYAVADANA: Sorry? Whatever for? The goddess knew what she was doing. I can tell you that. Ha Ha! Being a horse has its points. (*Pause.*) I have only one sorrow.

BHAGAVATA: Yes?

HAYAVADANA: I have become a complete horse—but not a complete being! This human voice—this cursed human voice—it's still there!

How can I call myself complete? What should I do, Bhagavata Sir? How can I get rid of this human voice?

BHAGAVATA: I don't know what to advise you, Hayavadana.

HAYAVADANA: That's why I sing all these patriotic songs—and the National Anthem! That particularly! I have noticed that the people singing the National Anthem always seem to have ruined their voices, so I try. But—but—it—it doesn't seem to work. What should I do?

(*He starts to sob.*)

BOY: Don't cry, horse. Don't cry. Stop it now.

HAYAVADANA: No, I won't cry. The boy's right. What's the point of shedding tears?

BOY: Don't cry. You are nice when you laugh.

HAYAVADANA: No, I won't cry. I won't give up trying either. Come, little friend, let's sing the National Anthem together.

BOY: What is that?

BHAGAVATA: How could he? He has been brought up in a forest.

HAYAVADANA: Then sing some other song. Look, if you sing a song, I'll take you round on my back.

BOY (*excited*): Yes—please.

HAYAVADANA: Well, then, what are we waiting for? Get on my back. Quick.

(*The Bhagavata seats the child on the horse's back.*)

BOY: Hiyah—Hiyah—

HAYAVADANA: No, no. You sing first. Then we start.

BHAGAVATA: Sing, son.

(*The boy sings and the horse goes around in a slow trot.*)

BOY: Here comes a rider.
From what land O what land?
On his head a turban.
Sleep now, sleep now.
Why his chest
Red O red?
Why his eyes
Pebbles O pebbles?

Why his body
Cold O cold?
Where goes the horse?
Nowhere O nowhere.

(*As the song ends, the horse comes and stands in front of the Bhagavata.*)

HAYAVADANA: Mr Bhagavata Sir…

BHAGAVATA: Yes.

HAYAVADANA: It seems to me the rider described in the song is dead. I am right?

BHAGAVATA: Er—I think so—yes.

HAYAVADANA: Who could have taught this child such a tragic song?

BOY: Mother…

BHAGAVATA: What's there in a song, Hayavadana? The real beauty lies in the child's laughter, in the innocent splendour of that laughter. No tragedy can touch it.

HAYAVADANA: Is that so?

BHAGAVATA: Indeed. What can match a child's laughter in its purity?

HAYAVADANA: To be honest, Mr Bhagavata Sir, I have my doubts about this theory. I believe—in fact I may go so far as to say I firmly believe—that it's this sort of sentimentality which has been the bane of our literature and national life. It has kept us from accepting Reality and encouraged escapism. Still, if you say so, I won't argue. Come, child, let's have another song.

BOY: I don't know…

HAYAVADANA: Then sing the same song again.

BOY: You laugh first.

HAYAVADANA: Laugh again? Let me try. (*Tries to laugh.*) Ha Ha Ha! No, it's not easy to laugh—just like that.

BOY (*mimes whipping*): Laugh—laugh…

HAYAVADANA: All right. All right. I'll try again. Ha! Ha! Ha! Ha!—Huhhuh… Heahhh…

(*His laughter ends up as a proper neigh.*)

ALL: What's that?

BHAGAVATA: Hayavadana—Hayavadana…

HAYAVADANA: Heahhh…

(*His human voice is gone now. He can only neigh and leaps around with great joy.*)

BHAGAVATA: Careful—careful. Don't drop the child...

(*But the horse is too happy to listen. It prances around, neighing gleefully. The boy is also enjoying himself, singing bits of the song and urging the horse on.*)

BHAGAVATA: So at long last Hayavadana has become complete. (*To the Actors.*) You two go and tell the Revered Brahmin Vidyasagara that his grandson is returning home in triumph, riding a big, white charger.

ACTOR II: And the dolls?

BHAGAVATA: Throw them away. There's no further need for them.

(*The Actors go out with the dolls.*)

Unfathomable indeed is the mercy of the elephant-headed Ganesha. He fulfils the desires of all—a grandson to a grandfather, a smile to a child, a neigh to a horse. How indeed can one describe His glory in our poor, disabled words?

Come, Hayavadana, come. Enough of this dancing. Our play is over and it's time we all prayed and thanked the Lord for having ensured the completion and success of our play.

(*Hayavadana comes and stands by the Bhagavata. The Bhagavata helps the child down. At this point the curtain, with the fire painted on it—which has been there all the time—is dropped and Padmini, Kapila and Devadatta step forward and join the Bhagavata in prayer.*)

Grant us, O Lord, good rains, good crop,
Prosperity in poetry, science, industry and other affairs.
Give the rulers of our country success in all endeavours,
and along with it, a little bit of sense.